BUTTON UP

Secrecy and Deception in the
Nuclear Fuel Cycle

Dr. Ronald A. Hardert

Order this book online at www.trafford.com
or email orders@trafford.com

Most Trafford titles are also available at major online book retailers.

Printed in the United States of America.

ISBN: 978-1-4907-2223-8 (sc)
ISBN: 978-1-4907-2224-5 (hc)
ISBN: 978-1-4907-2225-2 (e)

Library of Congress Control Number: 2013923384

Trafford rev. 02/22/2014

 www.trafford.com

North America & international
toll-free: 1 888 232 4444 (USA & Canada)
fax: 812 355 4082

"To the truth-tellers and the future of humanity."

Contents

Acknowledgments ix
Prologue xi

Chapter 1. Introduction: Costs of Secrecy
in the Nuclear Fuel Cycle..1
    Introduction.. 2
    The Tragedy in Japan 2
    Questioning Nuclear Technology 6
    Health Effects... 8
    Higher Economic Costs 9
    Nuclear Terror.. 11
    Nuclear Secrecy and Deception 12
    Regulatory Failure 13
    Radioactive Waste 14
    Waste Storage 15
    Cancer.. 16
    Additional Problems with Nuclear Electric 17
    Nuclear Weapons Issues.. 18
    Continuing Health Effects near Chernobyl 21
    The Cleanup at Fernald... 23
    Global Nuclear Fears 25
    References 27
Chapter 2. Environmental Problems in
the Nuclear Fuel Cycle: Fernald and Chernobyl.......................31
    Introduction... 31
    Developments within the US Nuclear Weapons Complex........................ 33
    Background on Fernald 37
    The Soviet Nuclear Waste Legacy 47
    References 50
Chapter 3. Nuclear Secrecy and Deception at the Fernald Plant.......54
    Introduction... 54
    The DOE Weapons Complex and Fernald 56
    Theory and Method... 59
    Deception and Secrecy at Fernald... 61
    Possible Deception on the National Level..................................... 66

Legal Problems at Fernald and Rocky Flats.............................69
What Happens If We Continue To Go Nuclear.........................73
References 78

Chapter 4. Psychosocial Effects of Secrecy
at Fernald and Chernobyl 83
Introduction...83
Voices from Fernald...83
Interviews: Being There...84
Nuclear Nightmares 92
Voices from Chernobyl* 93
Nuclear Skepticism..103
Death in Slow Motion..105
References 109

Chapter 5. Regulatory Failure at Fernald,
Chernobyl, and Fukushima 111
Introduction...111
Technological Civilization and the Legitimation Crisis..........112
Scope and Methods..116
Environmental Crime and the US Legitimation Crisis 119
Data Analysis: the United States and Canada 122
Nuclear Activism..123
Data Analysis: Post-Chernobyl Interviews 128
Western Europe..129
Eastern Europe 131
Crisis of Authority at Fukushima...139
References 141

Chapter 6. Alternatives to the Nuclear Fuel Cycle 147
Introduction...147
What Can Be Done to Shut Down the Nuclear Fuel Cycle?...148
How to Limit Global Warming Without Turning to Nuclear Power? 149
Affinity Groups Speak to Power 151
References 152

Epilogue...153
Appendix A 157
Appendix B 162
Subject Index 165
Name Index 173

ACKNOWLEDGMENTS

With grateful thanks to all who helped us along the way:

For their courage and inspiration, Professor and Mrs. Mark Reader, Dr. Helen Caldicott, Stewart Udall, Manny Pino, Lisa and Ken Crawford, Dr. Alice Stewart, Karen Silkwood, Dr. Rosalie Bertell, Dr. John Gofman, Dr. Roger Axford, Dr. Carl Johnson, Dr. Vasant Merchant, Charles and Emily Young, Dr. William Freudenburg, Dr. Kathy and David Schwarz, Melody Baker, Carol and Robert Kurth, Linda Hardert, Felice and Jack Cohen-Joppa, Dr. Austin and Marion Jones, Dr. Karl Z. Morgan, Don Hancock, Debbie McQueen, Lynn Bylow and Dr. Susan L. Maret.

For editing and proofreading, Dr. Mary R. Laner, Richard Everett, Dr. Paul Perry, Loyal Jones, Dr. Dennis Jacobs, Dr. David Krieger, and the Trafford Copy Editing Team.

For copy work, printing, and photos, Priscilla Hoskins, William Masters, Jack Borgman, and Norm Grant.

For word processing, Sandra Balistreri and Amanda Williams.

The Author

Key Words/Phrases: Public Health, Nuclear Secrecy and Deception, Peace, Economics, Environment, Humanities, Urban Geography, Public Policy, Community, Social Problems.

PROLOGUE

Social Consequences of Nuclear Secrecy

The world has achieved brilliance without conscience.
Ours is a world of nuclear giants and ethical infants.

—General Omar N. Bradley (1896-1981)

My colleague, friend and mentor, Dr. Mark Reader, and I published <u>Atom's Eve: Ending the Nuclear Age</u> in 1980. Since then, we published several journal articles and a major social problems textbook dealing with energy, technology, and society. Dr. Reader contributed many creative ideas to <u>Button Up</u>, then turned to successful watercolor painting after his retirement from Arizona State University. We are happy to say that Mark and I were able to combine many of our thoughts in this prologue; and, I wanted to acknowledge his contributions.

This book is as much about personal and community empowerment as it is about those technologies that shape our lives. In this work, we observe that even when they seemingly succeed, certain tools and techniques that characterize modern society can undermine it. And, as they do, they can create the circumstances in which individuals and small communities of people emerge as the authors and heroes of their own future.

In developing this thesis, we not only try to explain why modern technologies—from the use of chemicals and nuclear reactors to genetically engineered sheep—invariably fail to deliver on their promises of a better life for those they supposedly serve but, as importantly, why they eventuate in a series of legitimation (i.e., authority) crises for those who promote them. Thus, the Old

Paradigm of high technology must finally give way to the New Paradigm of less destructive, appropriate, and alternative technology.

Our analysis of the relationship between technics and human freedom is drawn from two major sources. From the critics of modern technology, we borrow the twin notions that people create themselves and their cultures through the tools and techniques they inherit or invent, and that, insofar as they do, the present-day environmental crisis may be regarded as the perceived need for past and present societies to introduce new and ever more dangerous technologies in order to support increasing numbers of people using and abusing most of the world's finite resources. In this regard, then, we share the outlook of those skeptics of modernity who view civilization itself as a hierarchically organized, progressively destructive, wealth-producing machine which must, but simply cannot, be governed in the future given the advent of those twenty-first century technologies of mass extermination that define it.

The second part of our inquiry is drawn from our continuing involvement in the peace and social justice movements and in the global grassroots response to an accelerating number of technological disasters in the oil, chemical, and nuclear industries. Indeed, it is to the many victims of modern technology that we owe our understanding that no matter what their immediate causes, technological accidents—such as those suffered at Seveso, Three Mile Island (TMI), Bhopal, Chernobyl, Prince William Sound, the Gulf of Mexico, the Shetland Islands, and in the space industry— simultaneously account for the demonizing as well as liberating politics of our time. Thus, in focusing upon the politics of nuclear contamination at the Fernald (Ohio) nuclear weapons plant, upon the Chernobyl nuclear electric station disaster, and upon the Fukushima tragedy, we are equally interested in problems that have arisen on both ends of the nuclear fuel cycle, military and civilian.

This book began as a study of the Fernald nuclear weapons plant and the tragedy at Chernobyl (Kiev) and was expanded to include: persistent nuclear regulatory failure, bureaucratic "slippage," and various regime cover-ups. Regarding Fernald, the institutional failure involves primarily the US Department of Energy (DOE), while the issue of bureaucratic slippage is a more recent phenomenon related both to Fernald and more recently to Fukushima Daiichi. In America, the US Congress enacted changes in environmental laws that could let thousands of corporations (including government contractors) off the hook for cleaning up the pollution they caused. At Fukushima, officials failed to deliver water and emergency supplies to the town of Iwaki, not far from the stricken plant, resulting in angry protests. And at Chernobyl, similar regulatory failure, political deception, secrecy, and cover-ups occurred before and after the accident in 1986.

When most people think about pollution problems, the tendency is to see business and industry as the culprits and to see government agencies as the source of solutions in the form of regulations and enforcement. However, our research reveals that the regimes themselves were the source of nuclear problems at Fernald, Chernobyl, and Fukushima. For instance, numerous Fernald workers came forward with charges of unsafe working conditions, threats, and industry efforts to cover up earlier and continuing mistakes. Yet, when not simply disregarded, these workers had the veracity of their claims called into question by the DOE and its contractors. Similarly, due to the culture of secrecy, the existence of various technical and human problems was ignored for years at Chernobyl, before ultimately being acknowledged publicly. And the Fukushima plant was not built to withstand earthquakes or tsunamis of the scale that hit Eastern Japan.

Drawing upon social power theories of C. Wright Mills, Michel Foucault, and Jürgen Habermas, we investigate the actual behavior of the DOE and its contractors at Fernald, as well as the behavior of Soviet officials immediately after the accident at Chernobyl. This original research analyzes interview data from persons near Fernald and Chernobyl, including analyses of both official and unofficial documentation and sources.

In the case of Fernald, we draw upon articles published in Cincinnati newspapers beginning with the discovery of uranium and trichloroethylene in local water wells in 1984, in addition to a great deal of data on the plant itself, its contractors, the DOE, and the eventual cleanup. All this is discussed in terms of possible environmental crimes, cover-ups, political controversy, and the role of Fernald Residents for Environmental Safety and Health (FRESH) and Lisa Crawford in forcing the cleanup.

This volume provides a policy analysis not only of the Chernobyl and of the Fernald nuclear weapons plant but also of the entire US nuclear weapons complex. It also examines public responses to the political dynamics surrounding global nuclear issues, such as increased generation of nuclear electric. This is especially relevant in light of the renewed bomb testing and development of new tactical nuclear weapons by various countries around the globe, even in the face of problems related to the cleanup and safe storage of *older* nuclear waste.

Given its timeliness and relevance, this book might serve as both a primary and a supplementary text in courses on public policy, peace, humanities, the environment, social theory, and social problems internationally. And, for the same reasons, the book may have wide public appeal, especially for those who want to understand what led to Fukushima. One further word by way of introduction: as in our past collaborations, wherever possible we have drawn upon the voices and experiences of many ordinary people in telling the story of the passage of contemporary society from a nuclear and chemical civilization into a more peaceful, ecologically sustainable, and democratic future.

What happens if we continue to go nuclear? The plan of this book is to demonstrate the consequences of having gone nuclear in the past. These problems include: the prohibitive costs of safe storage of nuclear waste and of building, maintaining, and eventually decommissioning all nuclear facilities; the secrecy and deception that surround all nuclear operations and facilities; the health effects of living near, and working within, nuclear power and nuclear weapons plants; psychosocial reactions to living in the nuclear age; authoritarian responses to the delegitimation of nuclear regimes; nuclear regulatory failures at home and abroad; and the vulnerability of nuclear facilities and processes to the threat of international terrorism.

Some people might say that this book tries to do too much and to cover too much ground. Actually, we aim to educate and activate the public about the connections between nuclear power and nuclear weapons and the need to abandon *both* to safeguard our future.

We say that the status quo is keeping students and the general public from "putting the pieces together," regarding the total nuclear threat to the global environment. Environmental scientists, authors, and instructors are encouraged to focus on one plant, one operation, one process, or one pollutant at a time. Thus, our "scientific" methods become inconclusive by design and our findings atheoretical. Anyone who understands the philosophy of science (e.g., Abraham Kaplan and Alfred North Whitehead) knows that this logical fallacy is called reductionism.

In order to counter this shortcoming, we decided to employ the interrelated themes of nuclear secrecy, deception, and the crisis of authority (Habermas et al.) by introducing major case studies as evidence that Fukushima does not stand alone. Following Habermas and the critical theorists, we hoped to develop a more democratic "Ideal Speech Community," where our readers and the nuclear elites would be on a more level playing field. Then, students and ordinary citizens would have some history and conceptual background for understanding modern nuclear issues. In other words, following the older scientific paradigm would have meant "knowing more and more about less and less." Further, in revising this manuscript over the past few years, we wanted to keep the book as readable as possible. Some recent nuclear books and articles are too narrow in focus and too technical for most audiences to comprehend. We advocate for an energy future that is sustainable, benign, and democratic.

Pitirim Sorokin, a famous social theorist at Harvard, once said that sociology had reduced its focus to "studying gnats and fleas on the great social elephant" (i.e., society itself). In writing this book on the entire nuclear fuel cycle and its problems, we have attempted to reverse that tendency. The focus on Fernald and Chernobyl serves to legitimate the safety (i.e., policing) functions of nuclear whistle-blowers all along the fuel cycle and strengthens the argument for getting members of the public onto all oversight nuclear safety boards, both nationally and globally. While focusing on Fernald, similar instances of cover-ups and whistle-blower attempts along the fuel cycle can also be used to bolster the case for public regulation, especially after Fukushima.

The coauthors: Ron Hardert and Mark Reader

CHAPTER 1

Introduction: Costs of Secrecy in the Nuclear Fuel Cycle

I think that we must understand that each time we introduce a new bit of technology, we invent, at the same time, a specific accident. The invention of the ship was the invention of the shipwreck. The invention of atomic electricity was the invention of Chernobyl.

—Paul Virilio (Post Modern, French theorist)

NUCLEAR FUEL CYCLE

1

Introduction

This introduction presents an update on recent developments in the nuclear fuel cycle so that we can examine the serious consequences inherent in the nuclear electric and weapons options. Nuclear power, for example, can no longer be regarded as "clean" energy, despite the claims of politicians and the utilities.

The Tragedy in Japan

Before this volume was completed, a 9.0 magnitude earthquake and related tsunami hit the east coast of Japan. The next day, March 12, 2011, nine Japanese nuclear reactors were placed under states of emergency—three at Fukushima Daiichi, three at Fukushima Daini, and three at Onagawa. All are located north-northeast of Tokyo, and all are the earlier type boiling water reactors. The station was designed to withstand a powerful earthquake and also a tsunami, but not the two occurring together.

Three of the Daiichi reactors were in critical condition immediately after the earthquake when the plants lost normal electric power and backup diesel power needed to cool down the reactors. Mass evacuations followed a hydrogen explosion in a containment building covering one of the three reactors. On March 13, 2011, the Associated Press reported a "probable partial meltdown" at a second Daiichi reactor. On March 14, a nonoperating fourth reactor caught fire and released additional radiation. By March 17, the *Los Angeles Times* reported that many persons isolated by the tsunami near the Daiichi facility were unable to escape the increasing levels of radiation. Authorities and others were simply afraid to help them. Almost twenty thousand Japanese were reported dead or missing by September 2011.

In all the chaos and panic that followed, much of the official worry centered on Reactor 3 at Daiichi because it was fueled with MOX, a mixed oxide combining uranium and highly toxic plutonium. By early March 28, CNN announced, and the *Arizona Republic* (2011) confirmed, that plutonium had been discovered in water outside one of the reactors, suggesting a breach of containment. With loss of reactor core containment, nuclear technology would have to be carefully reconsidered. The disaster in Japan has underlined the dangers of nuclear power (Robinson, March 16, 2011).

As we continued writing, the consequences of the Fukushima accident had begun to accumulate. Yukiya Amano, head of the UN's International Atomic Energy Agency (IAEA), described the accident as extremely serious. Fires, explosions, three partial meltdowns, and numerous radioactive leaks struck four of the six units at the Daiichi plant. "With its mangled machinery and partly melted reactor cores, bringing the complex under control is a monstrous job," reported the Associated Press on March 22. Radiation from the tsunami-damaged plant caused Tokyo's tap water to exceed safe-drinking standards for infants, and levels of radioactive iodine were more than twice what is considered safe for babies. By March 27, Japan's government admitted a series of mistakes by the Daiichi plant operator. For instance, workers were sent into the plant without protective footwear, resulting in two workers suffering skin burns when they stepped into water that was ten thousand times more radioactive than levels normally found near reactors. On March 28, a Tokyo Electric Power Company (TEPCO) spokesperson reported that a new test had found radiation levels hundred thousand times above normal (Associated Press, 2011). Robots were used later to confirm the high radiation levels (Yamaguchi, April 19, 2011).

Further consequences of the Fukushima accident include: the Swiss government imposing an immediate freeze on plans to build and replace nuclear power plants, Germany's decision to stop using nuclear energy because of its inherent risks (Baetz, March 27, 2011), and the sudden realization that property and liability insurance does not cover nuclear calamities (Wiles, March 27, 2011). In the event of a nuclear accident, the potential catastrophe is so large as to be almost immeasurable. Yet Iran began loading fuel rods into its first nuclear power plant, scheduled to be operating soon (Riyadi, 2010: A3).

Thus, the Fukushima Daiichi accident became the worst nuclear crisis Japan had faced since the World War II bombing of Hiroshima and Nagasaki. It was also the first time that such a serious nuclear threat had been raised since the Chernobyl nuclear power plant explosion in 1986. Exposure to such high levels of radiation can cause radiation poisoning, resulting in substantial damage to human and animal tissue, premature aging, and possible death. Prolonged exposure to lower radiation levels is also associated with increased risk of ill health, in general (Kotlabai, 2005).

Later, it was discovered that Unit 1 at Fukushima had been damaged more severely than originally thought (Yamaguchi, May 13, 2011). Newer data revealed that the water level in the core of Unit 1 was much lower than earlier suspected, leaving the fuel rods (that were still intact) fully exposed. These findings also indicate a greater than expected radioactive leak in that particular pressure vessel. This hindered the work to bring Unit 1 under control, as the president of TEPCO resigned in disgrace (Kageyama, May 21, 2011).

On June 26, 2011, the Japanese government held a public hearing on whether or not the reactor in Sage Prefecture should be the first of the nation's nuclear plants to be reactivated after the Daiichi disaster (Ozawa, 2012: 7). This was billed as a chance to gauge local opinion about nuclear power. Yet the hearing turned out to be less of a public forum and more of a piece of badly orchestrated political theater. On company orders, employees of Kyushu Electric Power sent in e-mails pretending to be citizens urging restarting of the reactor (Ozawa, 2012: 8). Nuclear secrecy breeds deception.

Subsequently, the Japanese government, power companies, and some of the media cooperated to withhold information and downplay nuclear dangers. For instance, Tokyo officials delayed releasing data from computer models that predicted the spread of radiation from the Fukushima plant. As Yoichi Funabashi, leader of the Independent Investigation Commission on the Fukushima Daiichi Nuclear Accident, told the *Asahi Shimbun*, "The government later decided the public were still children who would panic if given the true information" (Ozawa, 2012: 8).

Meanwhile, Japanese citizens were doing their own research. *People* posted radiation measures online and learned about the relative dangers of cesium, strontium, and plutonium isotopes, internal and external radiation, and the difference between sieverts and Becquerels (more on these terms later). "It was the beginning of a grassroots movement that has reinvigorated activism in Japan and given birth to new forms of political resistance" (Ozawa, 2012: 8). However, the most powerful protest in Japan might be that of a solitary man, Naoto Matsumura. He is the Fukushima farmer, who has refused to leave his home well within the nuclear exclusion zone, a protest that has meant exposing himself and his farm animals to potentially lethal levels of radiation. Mr. Matsumura sees himself among the *hibakusha*, the "bombed ones" at Hiroshima and Nagasaki.

More recently, an internal audit has confirmed observers' concerns that many of the US Environmental Protection Agency's (USEPA) radiation monitors were out of service at the height of the Fukushima meltdown. This finding raises serious questions about the federal government's ability to respond to nuclear emergencies and to alert the public of their consequences (*Global Security Newswire*, December 21, 2011). Further, an April 19, 2012, report by the EPA Inspector General's Office (IG) casts doubt on the agency's controversial claims that radiation from Fukushima did not pose any public health threat on US soil, said Daniel Hirsh, a nuclear policy lecturer at the University of California, Santa Cruz (Guarino, April 23, 2012: 1).

The IG's report details problems with the EPA's "Rad Net" monitoring system. This web of detectors is intended to monitor environmental radioactivity in the United States to provide data for assessing public exposure and environmental impacts resulting from nuclear emergencies. The IG report says that at the time of the Fukushima crisis, "this critical infrastructure asset" was impaired because many monitors were broken and others had not undergone necessary filter changes in so long that they could not be used to detect accurately "real-time" radiation levels (Guarino, April 23, 2012: 2). In addition, advocacy groups charged that repeated EPA statements that Fukushima fallout on US soil was far below "any level of concern" were misleading, given that the agency data showed it had detected radiation levels in the US milk and rainwater well above its own regulatory limits for drinking water.

Despite our reservations regarding the quality of USEPA monitoring processes, radioactive isotopes I-131, Cs-134, or Cs-137, products of uranium fission, were measured at approximately 20 percent of 167 sampled National Atmospheric Deposition Program monitoring sites in North America after the Fukushima accident on March 12, 2011. Technically speaking, samples were analyzed for the period of March 8 through April 5 and calculated 1- or 2-week radionuclide deposition fluxes at thirty-five sites from Alaska to

Vermont ranged from 0.47 to 5,100 Bq per square meter during the sampling period of March 15 through April 15, 2011. Yet no fission-product isotopes were measured in National Atmospheric Deposition samples obtained during March 8-15, 2011, *prior to the arrival of contaminated air* in North America (Wetherbee, Debey, Nilles, Lehemann, and Gay, 2012).

Dr. Kiyoshi Kurokawa, MD, chair of the Health and Global Policy Institute, received the 2012 Scientific Freedom and Responsibility Award from the American Association for the Advancement of Science (AAAS). Dr. Kurokawa was honored in February 2013 "for his contribution to remarkable stewardship of an independent investigation into the causes of the Fukushima catastrophe" and "for his courage in challenging some of the most ingrained conventions of Japanese government and society" (AAAS, 2012). The AAAS (2012) said that the investigation "was frank in its condemnation of the negligence leading to the accident, the many errors committed following the first signs of trouble at the plants, and the failure to take a range of protective steps at a nuclear facility with known risk factors." The report identified failures resulting from decisions made by the power plant operator (TEPCO), the government, the regulators, and even Japanese society itself.

Questioning Nuclear Technology

Professor Mark Reader, a political theorist, published a highly prescient op-ed in the *Los Angeles Times*, March 27, 1989. He said,

"The prime difficulty with nuclear power today is the same as it was before the Three Mile Island reactor accident . . . A radiation-producing energy source is simply ungovernable by any ordinary human measure. This is true whether one thinks about fission-produced electricity or bombs."

Dr. Reader went on to say that several challenges arise for any society dependent on the fissioned atom. In summary:

1. We must find a way to protect more of the Earth's limited freshwater supplies and arable land from radioactive contamination.

2. We must insulate ever-changing social and ecological systems from unwanted interactions with dangerous and accumulating radioactive wastes.
3. We must find a way to offset the many physical and mental health problems that emerge in the aftermath of "unscheduled" releases of radioactive materials anywhere along the overlapping nuclear fuel and arms networks.
4. We need to ask if there is a way to justify to an increasingly skeptical public the morality of randomly passing on cancer deaths, cancer incidence, and radiation-related birth defects to innocent persons over the generations.
5. We must reduce the often disastrous consequences of human error within the nuclear weapons and fuel systems without passing on life or death decisions to equally fallible, and often less flexible, computers.
6. We need to halt the proliferation of thermonuclear and biochemical weapons, as well as the antidemocratic imperatives they engender, by severing atomic weapons production from the commercial nuclear power industries.

Professor Reader further argued that even if we manage to accomplish all these goals, we still need to shield nonnuclear critics from economic, social, and political reprisals so that their warnings can be used to forestall predictable disasters in the future.

Respected environmental groups, such as the Physicians for Social Responsibility and the Worldwatch Institute, caution that the world may be awash in plutonium in the very near future as nuclear nations reprocess highly toxic spent reactor fuel to either extend their energy supplies and/or make atomic bombs.

Thus, nuclear accidents, such as those at Fernald, Chernobyl, and Fukushima, tell citizens that in return for the Faustian promise of an infinite supply of energy, wealth, and military security, they must saddle their children with the *silent* killer—radiation. And so, decades after what might have been the beginning of the end of the nuclear age (see Reader's *Atom's Eve*, 1980), we may slip deeper into its nuclear nightmares, humiliated into accepting the rule of a nuclear elite that we alternately worship and dread.

Taking Einstein's injunction seriously—that we need to change our mode of thinking in order to survive the Atomic Age—probably requires us to abandon the nuclear "game" entirely and to link the quest for nuclear disarmament to the delivery of safe, local, and ecologically sound energy systems.

Fukushima tells us that the lessons of Fernald and Chernobyl remain as important as they always were. That is, we should (1) think about the nuclear fuel *cycle* in making energy choices and (2) stop demonizing critical thinking as it may prove essential for our common survival. Further, nonnuclear experts and whistle-blowers should be included in the nuclear regulatory process globally. Considering the many prior warnings the Japanese authorities had about the instability of the Fukushima reactors from nuclear critics, it is clear that electric company executives and government officials have used their near-monopoly control of information about reactor performance to override the public good whenever critics have raised questions about reactor and fuel cycle safety (Glionna and Hall, 2011).

We hope that reading this book will help a post-Fukushima world more clearly understand why a nuclear-free civilization is imperative for the continuance of human health and happiness.

Health Effects

Regarding health effects associated with the nuclear fuel cycle, recent research results are informative. In 2007, the German Register of Child Cancer gathered data from regions near twenty-one of their reactors or former reactors. These scientists discovered that children under the age of five, living near nuclear power (electric) stations, contracted leukemia at a rate 60 percent higher than the German national average (see Appendix A, pp. 159-163). Given similar findings at all twenty-one German power stations, a radiation-linked cause is highly likely in every case.

In Russia, the recent health effects research is even more startling. Alexey Yablokov et al. (2010) found that nearly 1 million people globally have died from radiation exposure released by the 1986 Chernobyl nuclear (reactor) disaster. These authors examined more than five thousand published articles, mostly written in Slavic language and never before available in English.

Yablokov et al. explain that the two explosions at Chernobyl reactor number four tore the top from the reactor and its containment building and exposed the reactor core. The resulting fire sent a plume of radioactive fallout over large parts of the Western Soviet Union, Europe, and the Northern Hemisphere. Large areas of the Ukraine, Belarus, and Russia had to be evacuated. Further, nations outside the Former Soviet Union received large doses of radioactive fallout, especially Norway, Sweden, Denmark, Finland, Yugoslavia, Bulgaria, Austria, Romania, Greece, and parts of the United Kingdom and Germany. Radioactive fallout from Chernobyl reached the United States and Canada 9 days after the disaster.

Yablokov and his coauthors found that radioactive emissions from the damaged reactor once believed to be 50 million curies may have been as great as 10 billion curies or two hundred times greater than the initial estimate. Little research on Chernobyl health effects in the United States has been conducted, but one study by the Radiation and Public Health Project found that in the early 1990s, a few years after the Chernobyl meltdown, thyroid cancer in Connecticut children had nearly doubled.

It is interesting to note what has happened to the "liquidators," who are the approximately 830,000 people who were in charge of extinguishing the fire at Chernobyl and deactivating and cleaning up the site. Initially, the World Health Organization (WHO) and the IAEA estimated that only thirty-one people had died among the liquidators. Yablokov et al. found that by 2005, between 112,000 and 125,000 liquidators had perished.

Higher Economic Costs

Another issue of concern is the ever-higher *costs* associated with the nuclear energy and nuclear weapons, in general. Mark Clayton, writing in *The Christian Science Monitor* (August 9, 2009: 35), argues that the road to nuclear energy has been a bumpy ride.

> "In 1974, President Nixon announced Project Independence—a plan to build 1,000 nuclear stations. But

of the 253 reactors eventually ordered by the US electric industry, 71 were canceled before construction began, according to a tally by the antinuclear group Beyond Nuclear.

Of the 182 construction permits granted by the government commissions, 50 were abandoned in construction with billions in investment lost and 27 were closed before their 40-year leases expired—including the Three Mile Island plant's Unit 2."

Mr. Clayton explains that tiny New Hampshire Electric Cooperative, which had purchased only 2 percent of the new Seabrook nuclear power plant's generating output, produced the nation's highest electric rates and went into bankruptcy. This calamity was echoed nationwide. Several government-owned power companies, for example, the Washington Public Power System, eventually went bankrupt. Other investor-owned utilities, such as Long Island Lighting Company and Consumers Power, almost went under. Whether a nuclear project defaults depends on numerous factors, the most important being where costs of new construction are headed (Randazzo, 2010).

Although President Obama would like to build two additional nuclear power stations in the near future (*Arizona Republic*, 2010: A3), no nuclear electric plants are under construction yet because the potential owners have not secured federal licenses or loan guarantees. New guarantees in coming years could leave US taxpayers picking up the tab if nuclear utilities defaulted on their loans. And in the 1970s and 1980s, nuclear industry bailouts cost US taxpayers and ratepayers in excess of $300 billion in 2006 dollars, according to three independent studies cited by the Union of Concerned Scientists (UCS) (Clayton, August 9, 2009: 34). "You want to talk about bailouts—the next generation of new nuclear power (plants) would be Fannie Mae in spades," says Mark Cooper, senior fellow at Vermont Law School's Institute for Energy and the Environment (Clayton, 2009: 34). "Even if no loans were defaulted on, nuclear still would be too expensive," Cooper says.

To put it more bluntly, Peter Bradford, a former member of the Nuclear Regulatory Commission (NRC), argues, "Funding nuclear power on anything like the scale of one hundred plants over the next 20 years would involve an *intolerable level of risk* (italics added) for taxpayers because that level of new nuclear reactors would require just massive federal loan guarantees." Wind power also has a sizable up-front capital cost, but wind's *lifetime* cost is roughly one-third less than current estimates for nuclear power. Whether bomb plants or power plants, one constant in the nuclear business is that profits are privatized, costs are public, and risks are basically permanent (Clayton, 2009).

Nuclear Terror

Another serious problem contained within the nuclear fuel cycle is the potential for nuclear terrorism (Reader, 1980). This threat recently occurred in a terrorist hit against a likely nuclear site in Pakistan (Shah, *Lexington Herald-Leader*, October 24, 2009: A9). There are other possible "incidents" lurking within the fuel cycle. For instance, in a popular magazine, Rene Chun (2003: 64 ff) interviews a former nuclear security worker, and now whistle-blower, at the Indian Point nuclear power plant located 24 miles north of New York City. On September 11, 2001, American Airlines Flight 11 flew over Indian Point before it slammed into the north tower of the World Trade Center. The question arises, did the terrorists know the greater potential for fatalities at Indian Point and deliberately ignore it, due to the *symbolic* value (for them) of hitting the World Trade Center?

Foster Zeh, the former security supervisor at Indian Point, describes the plant as "an accident waiting to happen" and a facility vulnerable to terror. Government and company officials say the plant's radioactive waste is safe, but Mr. Zeh tells a different story. "The chances of an attack on Indian Point are tremendously high," says Zeh. His major concerns revolve around: lack of thought in the plant's defensive plan, fatigued guards who work too much overtime, poor training of the guards, but mostly the plant's spent-fuel pools that are considerably softer targets than the concrete-contained reactors. None of the three waste storage pools have containment domes, and the pools' waste includes huge amounts of cesium-137—a volatile radioactive isotope. Release of radiation from the pools would render New York and New Jersey a toxic wasteland

(Caldicott, 2006: 74). It is no wonder that Indian Point heads the list of the ten US nuclear power sites most at risk (*Newsweek*, 2011, March 28 and April 4: 4).

Chun (2003: 142) goes on to explain, "These pools weren't designed to resist attack . . . Draining a spent-fuel pool is within the capabilities of a well-trained paramilitary unit." And the spent-pool technology was put in place in the 1970s to hold a relatively small amount of extremely toxic material. They are now overlooked, holding five times more waste than is appropriate. Further, the NRC's own studies show that a spent-fuel *fire* is also a distinct possibility. Just take away the (cooling) water, and the fuel will ignite and burn spontaneously. Still, the official opinion at NRC is that Indian Point's three cooling pools are "completely secure" (Chun, 2003: 142).

Nuclear security expert Pete Stockton (Chun, 2003: 144) calls Mr. Zeh a hero. And he backs up Zeh's allegations about sleeping and overweight guards, who "can't shoot straight and . . . would fold like a card table upon hearing an alarm." Mr. Stockton also agrees with Zeh that the mock attack drills at Indian Point are rigged to make the plant *seem* secure. Stockton confirms all of Zeh's criticisms of Indian Point and adds that virtually every other nuclear power plant in the United States is an "indefensible target." Terrorists attacked the World Trade Center in 1993 with a conventional car bomb that left six persons dead. A small, crudely fabricated nuclear device with an unpredictable yield could have toppled the twin towers (Hughes, 1996: 56).

Nuclear Secrecy and Deception

At this point, it is probably clear that the threat of nuclear terror contributes to nuclear secrecy and deception (see Chapter 3) and creates an authoritarian society that is prone to regulatory failure (see Chapter 5) at the plants themselves.

Fear of nuclear terror and "bad press" (media effects) can then lead to stereotyping (negative labeling) of highly competent nuclear scientists, workers, and honest whistle-blowers (see Appendix B: p 164), such as Foster Zeh. This generalization seems to hold for activity at "both ends" of the nuclear fuel cycle—electric and weapons. The end effect of this mini-theory of how nuclear elites handle criticism of the fuel cycle is to *demonize* nuclear scientists, workers, and especially whistle-blowers who have to deal with the psychosocial effects of negative labeling. Scientists whose research findings threaten "protocol" lose grant money, and whistle-blowers are placed on "administrative leave." Thus, no positive changes occur within the system that might transform nuclear realities into something that could bode well for humanity's future.

Regulatory Failure

The reasons for which we wrote this book are pretty well summed up in the words of Mr. Don Hancock, director of the Nuclear Waste Safety Project of the Southwest Research and Information Center in Albuquerque, New Mexico. For instance, regarding nuclear whistle-blowing, in general, Hancock says,

> "I think there's more and more feeling that scientists are not really concerned about some of the things they should be concerned about. . . . Our government system and scientific system really are not geared to think about and protect future generations. The political system operates on winning the next election."

Near the end of his interview, Mr. Hancock poses this important question:

> "How do we demystify the technical-scientific jargon, the computer models, etc., in a way that citizens can feel that it somehow relates to them, and that's this whole idea of let's have scientific criteria to judge the safety of the facility itself? And the second principle is how do we make people understand that this facility *will* affect them?"

Conditions at the Nevada Test Site seem to confirm Hancock's statements (Vartabedian, 2009). Over 41 years, the US government detonated 921 nuclear warheads underground at the test site located 75 miles northeast of Las Vegas. Each explosion deposited a toxic load of radioactivity into the ground. Some explosions deposited radiation directly into aquifers, and about one of eight explosions leaked radioactivity into the atmosphere when doors in the underground tunnels were blown off. Contamination from the test site has polluted about 1.6 trillion gallons of water, which the State of Nevada says would be worth as much as $48 billion today. "Because the contaminated water poses no immediate health threat," the DOE ranks Nevada at the bottom of its priority list for cleanup among the major sites in the US nuclear weapons complex (Vartabedian, 2009: A-11).

Radioactive Waste

Over the last six decades, radioactive waste has piled up at nuclear plants all over the United States, and about 21 percent of the electricity used in America comes from nuclear electric stations that are direct descendants of the bombs dropped at Hiroshima and Nagasaki. President Obama has called for a new generation of nuclear power plants (Dokoupil, 2010: 8). But since plans to store the nation's high-level waste at Nevada's Yucca Mountain have been all but abandoned, Obama is forcing states that want nuclear reactors to keep that waste within their borders—not a popular idea since the TMI meltdown and the tragedy at Chernobyl.

Thirty years ago, a generation of safe energy advocates warned that nuclear power and nuclear weapons were not immaculately conceived. Dr. Helen Caldicott, a Boston pediatrician and antinuclear activist, was one of these voices. In a recent address on the medical and ecological consequences of nuclear power, Dr. Caldicott (2005) pointed out the fact that the nuclear power industry is promoting nuclear electric as a panacea in the reduction of global-warming gases. In fact, she said, if nuclear power were to replace fossil fuels on a large scale globally, it would be necessary to build two thousand large 1,000-megawatt nuclear reactors. Further, to replace all fossil fuel-generated electricity today with nuclear power, there is only enough economically viable uranium to fuel these world-be reactors for 3 or 4 years. Besides, Belgium, Germany, Spain, and Sweden have decided to phase out their *operating* reactors due to a litany of problems now associated with the licensing, building, and operating of these types of plants.

According to Dr. Caldicott, the negative aspects of increased nuclear electric generation include the costs of uranium enrichment, the massive liability involved in a nuclear accident, the enormous costs of decommissioning all existing and new reactors (Pasqualetti, 1990), and the great expense incurred in the transportation and storage of high-level radioactive waste for at least 250,000 years.

The prevailing ethic promoted by the utilities says that nuclear power is "emission-free." The truth is quite different. Nuclear power stations normally release small but measurable amounts of radiation. And even very low nuclear doses pose a risk of cancer over a human lifetime, according to the National Academy of Sciences (Caldicott, 2005). The academy, therefore, is now concerned about radiation levels allowed at abandoned reactors and other nuclear sites. Some antinuclear advocates argue that stringent regulations are needed when cleaning up abandoned nuclear sites and considering health risks near nuclear power plants. Thus, there is virtually no radiation dose that is completely safe (Maugh II, 2005). In connection with these findings, it should be noted that cancer, not heart disease, is now the leading cause of death in America (Sherman, 2005). And for the first time in the US history, those younger than 85 years will die of cancer before any other cause. Clearly, governmental agencies are failing to protect public health both here and abroad.

Waste Storage

While politicians and media are arguing for more nuclear power stations, we still need a long-term solution for the problem of medium- and high-level nuclear waste storage. The subject of massive quantities of radioactive waste accumulating at 435 global nuclear reactors is rarely, if ever, addressed by the nuclear industry. According to Dr. Caldicott (2005), the typical 1,000-megawatt reactor produces 33 tons of thermally hot, intensively radioactive waste per year. More than 80,000 metric tons of highly radioactive waste sits in cooling ponds next to the 104 operating US nuclear power plants, awaiting transport to yet-to-be-named storage facilities. Much more nuclear waste accumulates at reactor sites in France, Russia, Japan, and elsewhere. The long-term storage of radioactive waste is an immense, and perhaps insoluble, social, political, and environmental problem.

Cancer

According to Dr. Caldicott (2005), the incubation time for cancer is 5-50 years, following exposure to ionizing radiation. Children, elders, and individuals with weakened immune systems are many times more sensitive to the malignant effects of radiation than other persons. Iodine-131, which was released at Chernobyl and at TMI in Pennsylvania, is radioactive for 23 weeks, and it bio-concentrates in leafy vegetables and milk. Iodine-131 enters the human body via the stomach and lungs, where it can later induce thyroid cancer. In Belarus, north of the Ukraine, more than two thousand children have had their thyroids removed because of cancer, a situation never before recorded in pediatric literature. Plutonium-239 is so toxic that one-millionth of a gram is carcinogenic, and on inhalation, it causes lung cancer. Plutonium, which remains seriously radioactive for 500,000 years, can cause testicular cancer and induce genetic diseases in future generations.

A study published in November 2005 in *Radiation Research* by the US and Russian scientists blamed excess cancers in the Ural Mountains in Central Russia on chronic exposures to low doses of radiation leaked from a weapons factory 50 years ago. *Science* magazine called the new report—along with a large-scale study revealing an elevated cancer risk in nuclear industry workers around the world—"the strongest direct evidence yet of chronic, low-dose health effects."

In spite of the negatives noted above, the George W. Bush Administration planned America's first production of plutonium-238 since the Cold War, stirring debate over the risks and benefits of this deadly material (Broad, 2005). "The real reason we are starting production is for national security," stated Timothy A. Frazier in an earlier interview. Frazier was the head of radioactive power systems at the DOE. He vigorously denied that any newly produced plutonium would involve the production of nuclear arms, satellites, or weapons in space.

Along similar lines, with uranium prices high and with support from President Obama, uranium miners in the United States are going back to work. The downside of uranium miners going underground relates to radon gas, a by-product of mining uranium. When radon gas is inhaled in the mines, it gradually damages lung cells, increasing the risk of lung cancer and related lung diseases (Piño, 1995). A 2000 report from the National Institute of Occupational Health concludes that workers who mined uranium during the 1940s through the 1970s died from lung cancer at a rate six times greater than expected. Because it can take decades for cancer to manifest itself, in many cases the mining company's liability for worker's compensation has expired, and the federal government has had to pay millions of dollars in damages.

With its nuclear legacy in mind, the Navajo Nation banned uranium mining and processing on the 17 million acres of tribal land, as well as on lands owned by Navajo families. The tribal council passed the ban and signed it into law in April 2005 (Paskus, 2005). Similarly, environmental groups in Colorado are opposed to locating a new uranium mill near the remote town of Paradox (*New Yorker*, 2010). The issue also has divided the community, and some people who oppose the mill have been physically threatened.

Additional Problems with Nuclear Electric

Other problems abound in the nuclear electric cycle. For instance, advocates for sick nuclear workers say that new rules set by the US Department of Labor will hurt workers trying to collect money from a federal compensation program (Munger, 2005). The new regulations replace DOE authority in handling certain aspects of the compensation program. Some former nuclear workers fear that federal agencies may have thwarted congressional intent to compensate sick nuclear weapons' workers.

Also within the nuclear electric cycle, Dr. Rosalie Bertell, president of the International Institute of Concern for Public Health, continues to call attention to a possible cover-up at TMI in Pennsylvania. Now that the Cold War is over, Dr. Bertell (2005) has asked former President Jimmy Carter, a longtime promoter of nuclear energy, to come forward with all the facts related to the TMI accident in 1979. This includes a candid discussion of the initial radiation release at TMI and the radiation dose to the public. To date, President Carter has remained silent on this issue.

Prompted by a string of accidental radioactive discharges in the United States, federal monitors said in March 2006 (*Arizona Republic*) that they formed a task force to investigate spills at several nuclear power plants, including discharges at Palo Verde Nuclear Generating Station in Wintersburg, Arizona, as well as in Illinois and New York. At Palo Verde, work crews discovered tritium-laced water in an underground pipe vault near Unit 3. Tests confirmed that the water contained more than three times the acceptable amount of tritium, a by-product of nuclear power generation. Arizona Public Service Company is working with state and federal officials to pinpoint the source of the leak and to determine how far it has spread.

Similarly, the NRC missed warning signs that an Ohio nuclear power plant had a massive hole in its reactor head, because inspectors failed to notify officials at NRC headquarters of their findings (Associated Press, 2003). The plant had been shut down previously in February 2002, but 1 month later, a leak was discovered that had allowed boric acid to eat nearly through the 6-inch steel cap covering the plant's reactor vessel. *Sierra* Magazine (2010: 45) summarizes nuclear electric problems in the following excerpt:

> "Nuclear-power advocates rightly point out that nukes are a huge potential source of (mostly) carbon-free energy. Yet after 53 years of trying to make it work nuclear power remains expensive, dangerous, a security risk, and inextricably linked to a radioactive waste stream. Nor is it the carbon-free option it's purported to be, as uranium mining and fuel processing are a significant source of greenhouse-gas emissions. It's on cost alone, however, that the true folly of nuclear power becomes clear—it's so much more expensive than other energy options that it has been incapable of surviving without massive government and ratepayer subsidies."

Nuclear Weapons Issues

Recent problems and issues abound at the other end of the fuel cycle as well, that is, in the nuclear weapons arena. For instance, in

September 2005, a jury in Washington State awarded more than $4.7 million in damages to eleven pipe fitters who sued a contractor at the Hanford nuclear reservation, saying they were fired for speaking up about safety concerns (Hopkins, 2005). Now considered the most contaminated nuclear site in the nation, Hanford produced plutonium for nuclear weapons for more than 40 years. This 586-square-mile property in Southeastern Washington once hosted nine nuclear reactors, five separation plants, and hundreds of support facilities. By 1987, all the Hanford reactors were closed except the Columbia Generating Station, the only commercial nuclear power plant in the Northwest.

The Hanford site has more than 170 massive underground steel tanks filled with acids, solvents, and heavy metals, including the radioactive elements plutonium, cesium, strontium, and uranium. One hundred and forty of the storage tanks are 40-60 years old and considered "unfit for use." The original cleanup agreement called for the tanks to be purged within a few decades, but at current funding levels, it will take more than a century to empty them. In addition to the 53 million gallons of Hanford tank waste, untold amounts of radioactive and hazardous waste languish in unlined landfills, along with 450 billion gallons of liquid waste in ponds, ditches, and drain fields. The Hanford site has already contaminated 200 square miles of groundwater (Coyle, 1988).

In Idaho, failing tanks at the Idaho National Laboratory are leaking radioactive waste generated from nuclear weapons production into the groundwater. Chromium, tritium, and other contaminants have already been detected in the Snake River Plain Aquifer, the sole drinking water source for more than 300,000 residents of Eastern Idaho. It is feared that budget shortfalls will only make things worse in Idaho, perhaps leading to spills of PCBs (Polychlorinated biphenyls), uranium, plutonium, and hazardous chemicals, as well as preventing necessary equipment maintenance (Coyle, 1988).

Meanwhile, permit changes at the Waste Isolation Pilot Project (WIPP) in New Mexico have postponed shipments from Idaho and added to costs. And one long-planned "solution" to the problem, the proposed Yucca Mountain nuclear waste repository 90 miles northwest of Las Vegas, is beset with legal, logistic, and budgetary challenges, as well as a recently discovered underground fault. Thus,

Yucca Mountain may not open for at least another decade, if ever (Haber, 2010).

At Yucca Mountain, the proposed permanent home of 77,000 metric tons of high-level commercial and military nuclear waste, e-mails show that federal employees circumvented quality-assurance procedures (Associated Press, 2005a). Survey hydrologists may have made up "facts" and deleted "inconvenient" data to make the proposed nuclear waste repository looks more viable. Yucca Mountain was originally selected for possible waste storage due to its arid location, 90 miles northwest of Las Vegas in the Mojave Desert. Ironically, the main controversy over the site's safety now involves water leaks as groundwater pathways were discovered under the mountain in 2001. More recently, the US Congress seems to be looking at alternatives to nuclear waste storage at Yucca Mountain. Proponents of reprocessing nuclear waste say it could reduce the waste and eliminate the need for Yucca Mountain. But many nuclear experts say that reprocessing technology does not work. The practice was stopped in 1979 due to expense and the fact that the process generates a type of plutonium isotope that could be used in nuclear bombs.

Various lawsuits have been aimed at contamination generated from nuclear weapons plants. For instance, in October 1989, the DOE agreed to a $78 million settlement in a class-action suit representing 14,000 Fernald, Ohio residents over uranium pollution generated by that plant (Crawford, 2009). In November 2002, Pantex (Texas) Nuclear Plant contractor Neasan and Hauger settled for an undisclosed sum with plant neighbors claiming devalued property and contaminated groundwater. And in January 2004, a federal judge dismissed a lawsuit brought by 135 residents living within 10 miles of Paducah, Kentucky's Gaseous Diffusion Plant.

At Rocky Flats, crews decontaminating the former nuclear weapons plant discovered five radioactive "hot spots" outside the established cleanup area (Associated Press, 2005b). This discovery prompted decontamination contractor Kaiser Hill to expand soil cleanup around the site, known as the 903 Pad. At Rocky Flats, workers previously shaped plutonium into hockey-puck-sized spheres that were key components of nuclear triggers for igniting America's weapons of mass destruction. Now, the largest hazardous waste cleanup in the US history has entered its final stages. Rocky Flats "reservation," which is nearly half the size of Manhattan, is being turned into a wildlife refuge (Rosner, 2005).

Similarly, in 2002, Chernobyl was opened as a tourist attraction. Few tourists appeared in 2002, but by 2004 and 2005, almost nine hundred arrived each year. A 19-mile radius around Chernobyl has been mostly closed to the world since the plant's Number. 4 Reactor exploded on April 26, 1986, and hurled 180 metric tons of nuclear fuel into the atmosphere. But Chernobylinterinform, the zone's information agency, says its chaperoned tours do not carry health risks for tourists. The agency says this is because radiation levels there "have always been uneven." Also, most of the zone in question is far cleaner than it was in 1986 when radiation levels were strong enough to kill "even the trees." Still, the zone in Northern Ukraine has many more radioactive spots than those where tourists typically go (Chivers, 2005). Despite the design flaws of Chernobyl's Reactor Number 4, the three other reactors stayed in operation. A second reactor was taken out of service after a fire in 1991, but the last reactors remained in service until 2000.

Continuing Health Effects near Chernobyl

Regarding the continuing health effects of the accident at Chernobyl, the journal *Nature* reports that in Greece (2,800 km from Chernobyl), where radiation exposures were far lower than in areas closer to the crippled reactor, leukemia has been diagnosed at rates 2.6 times the norm in young people who were in the womb when Reactor Number 4 exploded (Elofson-Hurst, 2005). The report from Greece is the first to link the Chernobyl tragedy to increased leukemia incidence in children exposed to radiation *in utero*.

Further, the *Swiss Medical Weekly* (2005) has published findings from the Clinical Institute of Radiation Medicine and Endocrinology Research, Minsk, Belarus, showing a 40 percent increase in cancer between 1990 and 2000. These researchers used data from the Soviet National Cancer Registry, established in 1973. They compared the post-Chernobyl period with rates before the plant's accident. The authors also note that increases in breast cancer are happening *earlier* within populations in the more highly contaminated Vitebsk. This dose-related difference in the time lag for radiation-induced cancer is known from other studies and is most marked for breast cancer.

There are other health consequences related to the Chernobyl accident. The Belarusian association "Seeds of Life" reports a decline in the *general* health of children in the Bragin district of Belarus (Kotlabai, 2005). Further, the director of the Belrad Institute in Minsk reports that while 90 percent of the children in the contaminated fallout zones were healthy in 1985, only 20 percent of the children are healthy now. Curiously, the pathologies of the children at Minsk are not those expected to follow exposure to radiation. Instead of cancers, these children are displaying "old people's illnesses," such as cardiovascular illness and problems of the immune and digestive systems.

Since the 1940s, scientists have known that genes carry information from one generation to the next, and that genes gone "haywire" can cause cancer, diabetes, and other diseases. But scientists have also known that genes are not the entire story because identical twins—whose genes are identical—can have very different medical histories. One identical twin can be perfectly healthy, while the other develops schizophrenia or cancer, so the environment must play a significant role, not merely genes (Montague, 2005).

What is surprising is that health scientists are now revealing that those nongenetic, environmental effects can be passed from one generation to the next with far-reaching implications for human health. An area of study termed "epigenetics" is demonstrating that environmental influences can be inherited, even without any mutation in the genes themselves. In other words, the cancer you get today may have been caused by your father's exposure to radiation or chemicals 20 or 30 years ago, even though your father's genes were not altered by the earlier environmental exposure (Montague, 2005). Although the field of epigenetics is only about 20 years old, in 2004, the National Institutes of Health granted $5 million to Johns Hopkins Medical School in Baltimore to start the Center for Epigenetics of Common Human Disease. This is a small amount of money compared to the $5 billion advanced to the DOE for the cleanup at the Fernald weapons plant.

Fernald weapons plant about the time it stopped production in 1989.

The Cleanup at Fernald

From 1951 to 1988, the Fernald site produced uranium metals used in the production of nuclear weapons. According to the DOE, tons of radioactive contamination blew as far as 5 miles from the plant site. For more than a decade, the DOE has conducted an environmental remediation project at the site to address this historical contamination. As part of this project, thousands of tons of highly contaminated materials have been shipped off the Fernald property, while a much greater volume of materials with lower concentrations of contamination have been placed in a specially designed disposal facility located on the site. Meanwhile, groundwater was being pumped to the surface, treated to remove contaminants, and injected back to the aquifer.

At Fernald, the first shipment of high-level nuclear waste taken from the aging K-65 silos rolled out of the plant June 6, 2005 on its way to Texas (Klepal, 2005). The story of how this waste is ending up in Texas is interesting in and of itself. Apparently, no other state in the United States would take it. A failed attempt at *vitrification*— embedding the waste in molten glass—wasted tens of millions of tax dollars. Then a Utah waste handler withdrew from consideration after public outcry against dumping the waste containers in that state. The US government's plan for burying the waste in the Nevada desert fell apart when the state's attorney general threatened a lawsuit to keep the Fernald waste out of his state. Finally, Waste Central Specialists of Andrews, Texas, agreed to store the waste in one of its facilities, while it pursues a license to permanently dispose of it in that location.

Although the K-65 silo waste was the most radioactive material at Fernald, it was not thought to be terribly dangerous on the road since it was mixed with fly ash and concrete and was poured into steel canisters to harden for transport (Klepal, 2005). The first shipment of waste that left Fernald June 6, 2005 was only one of 2,100 shipments of similar material stored in the K-65 silos since the 1950s. These shipments reportedly represent the last major hurdle in a $4.4 billion cleanup being paid for by American taxpayers. As of August 1, 2005, 240 containers had been filled, and 134 containers had been shipped to Waste Central Specialists in Texas.

Other decontamination projects at Fernald include: *the water pits remedial action project*, wherein Fernald workers excavated 1 million tons of waste generated from the waste pits during the uranium foundry era; the *waste management project* that encompassed shipment of low-level liquid, mixed waste for incineration, treatment, and disposal of mixed waste soil, sludge, and debris, disposal of additional hazardous waste, and recycling and pollution prevention efforts; the *soil and disposal facility project*, which called for an on-site disposal facility to be closed in late 2005 and capped in early 2006; *decontamination and demolition,* in which Fernald dismantled 213 of the 259 plant structures and 106 of the 179 trailers; and the *aquifer restoration/waste water project* that will handle the site's groundwater cleanup operations from this point forward (FRESH News, 2005).

On Friday, November 19, 2004, Fernald Residents for Environmental Safety & Health, Inc., celebrated their 20-year anniversary with a dinner and other events at the Crosby Township Senior Center. One hundred people attended, and the evening began with the dinner, donated by the cleanup contractor, Fluor Fernald, and provided by Boston Butts of Ross, Ohio. The FRESH organization led by Lisa Crawford continues its efforts to get the Fernald facility cleaned up, to communicate with and educate the surrounding communities, and to advocate for responsible environmental restoration and public health and safety (FRESH News, 2005).

Although the Soviet Union *per se* is gone, the nuclear fears that fueled the Cold War have not disappeared (Lester, 2005). Recent polls indicate that most Americans think nuclear weapons are so dangerous that *no* country should have them, and a majority of Americans believe it is likely that global terrorists or some nuclear nation will use these weapons within the next 5 years.

Global Nuclear Fears

The stated goal of the US nuclear policy is to keep weapons-grade nuclear materials out of the hands of terrorists and hostile, "unstable" nations. In actuality, the United States is failing to sweep up weapons-grade nuclear materials that exist in forty countries (Montague, 2004). America has opened a "second nuclear age" by creating a new generation of smaller, "more usable" A-bombs, and despite the terrors of 9/11, the US government is still selling Westinghouse nuclear reactors to countries, such as China, that have announced plans to pass along the latest nuclear technology to countries like Pakistan. In the hands of any willing nation, nuclear power potentially equals nuclear weapons as we know from the examples of India, Pakistan, North Korea, Iran, among others (Montague, 2004).

By writing this book, we have asked the readers to avoid the reductionism of focusing upon the problem of only a few reactors at a time. Instead, we hope that readers will think of the nuclear fuel cycle in its entirety, not weapons plants *versus* civilian, nuclear electric plants. Conversely, within the global nuclear fuel cycle, we have used Fernald and Chernobyl as exemplars of what has happened throughout the cycle.

It seems to us that the nuclear question has been bogged down in a "misplaced concreteness," which, unless corrected, may have tragic consequences for people in this and future generations. The important issue in the nuclear debate is not whether isolated atomic reactors can be made safe, but rather what kind of lives people will be forced to live while they try to secure those reactors. It is only when people are worried, not so much about individual reactors and plants, but about the *entire* nuclear fuel cycle and its attendant problems that objections to nuclear power and weapons come into focus.

Sobered by these reflections, a growing number of people around the globe have begun to oppose *any* use of the fissioned atom as a way out of both energy and security problems. Atom-splitting, these persons maintain, creates more problems than it solves. And, they also say, there is no reason to believe that the inhuman demands of the so-called peaceful atom will be any different from, or less than, those already made by the atomic bomb.

Nobel laureate Hannes Alven, when considering the expansion of the nuclear fission option in 1974, noted that a large production of nuclear energy necessarily means the mass production of radioactive poisons in massive quantities (Reader, 1980). In other words, the greater the number of nuclear plants, the greater the number of radioactive transactions and occasions for breakdowns all along the nuclear fuel cycle. This includes the mining of uranium, generation of electricity, and the search for semipermanent repositories for the handling of atomic waste.

The nuclear fuel cycle has been called a death or cancer machine (Caldicott, 2006), because throughout the process, scientists are stirring up or manufacturing radioactive elements that are damaging to human health in this and future generations. The plutonium generated in the nuclear fuel cycle is the stuff with which hydrogen bombs are made, and the radioactive half-life of plutonium remains at 24,400 years. No one can guarantee that none of the hazardous substances produced in the world's military and civilian atomic programs will be lost, misused, or accidently released into our environment.

Accordingly, we urge our readers to join the global campaign to halt humanity's nuclear bondage by closing the nuclear fuel cycle at its source.

Given the work of people such as Helen Caldicott, Hazel Henderson, Barry Commoner, Amory and Hunter Lovins, Lewis Mumford, E. F. Schumacher, and many others, it should come as no surprise to learn that any energy choice is doomed to failure if it is based on unlimited growth strategies alone. Instead, a realistic energy policy must be based on conservation, greater energy efficiency, clean energy alternatives, and the rapid introduction of a peaceful, solar-based economy wherever possible.

References

AAAS. 2012. "Scientific Freedom and Responsibility Award." December 4.

Associated Press. 2003. "Inspectors failed to report problems at nuclear plant." *New Mexican*, October 22, p. A7.

Associated Press. 2005a. "House panel to subpoena Yucca Mountain worker." June 13, http://www.nytimes.com

Associated Press. 2005b. "Colorado nuclear waste has spread." *Arizona Republic*, September 3, p. A3.

Associated Press. 2011. "More hurdles impede emergency workers in Japan nuke crisis." March 28, p. A6.

Arizona Republic. 2010. "Obama backs loan plan for new nuclear plant." February 17, pp. A3 and A9.

Arizona Republic. 2011. "Toxic plutonium seeping into soil." March 29, p. A3.

Baetz, Jüergen. 2011. "Germany plans to quit using nuclear energy." *Arizona Republic*, March 27, p. A26.

Bertell, Rosalie 2005. "Three Mile Island cover-up: Dr. Rosalie Bertell's signed notarized statement." July 9, http://www.mothersalert.org/bertell.html

Broad, William J. 2005. "U.S. has plans to again make own plutonium." *New York Times*, June 27.

Caldicott, Helen. 2005. "The medical and ecological consequences of nuclear power." Presented to the 2005 NPT Review Conference, May 15, Globnet.

Caldicott, Helen. 2006. "Nuclear power's sick legacy." *International Journal of Humanities and Peace*, Vol. 22, No. 1, p. 74.

Chivers, C. J. 2005. "Chernobyl now tourist hot spot." *Arizona Republic*, June 19, p. A33.

Chun, Rene. 2003. "The China syndrome 2003." *Playboy*, May, Vol. 50, No. 5, p. 65ff.

Clayton, Mark. 2009. "The bumpy road to nuclear energy." *The Christian Science Monitor*, August 9, p. 35.

Coyle, D. 1988. *Deadly Defense: Military Radioactive Landfills.* New York: Radioactive Waste Campaign.

Crawford, Lisa. 2009. Telephone conversation regarding class-action suit. Fall.

Dokoupil, Tony. 2010. "Kentucky wants your nuclear waste." *Arizona Republic*, February 22, p. 8.

Elofson-Hurst, Susan. 2005. "Basic facts re nuclear power and Chernobyl." *Arizona Republic*, February 17.

FRESH News. 2005. "Projects." Summer, Vol. 34, pp. 2-3. Harrison, OH 45030.

Glionna, John M., and Kenji Hall. 2011 "Japanese drop politeness norm amid crisis." *Arizona Republic*, May 1.

Global Security Newswire, December 21, 2011.

Guarino, Douglas P. 2012. "Audit confirms EPA radiation monitors broken during Fukushima crisis." *Global Security Newswire*, April 23, p. 1.

Haber, Jim. 2010. "Yucca Mountain: Let's wear our laurels but not rest on them." *Desert Voices*, Vol. 23, No. 1, Spring, p. 1.

Hopkins, Mary. 2005. "Jury rules for 11 Hanford pipe fitters; $4.8 million awarded." *Tri-City Herald*, September 3, http://www.tri-cityherald.com

Hughes, David. 1996. "When terrorists go nuclear." *Popular Mechanics*, January, pp. 56-59.

Kageyama, Yuri. 2011. "Japan utility boss quits amid crisis." *Arizona Republic*, May 21, p. D1.

Klepal, Dan. 2005. "Waste starts leaving Fernald today." *Cincinnati Enquirer*, June 6, pp. A1-A9.

Kotlabai, Tatiana. 2005. "Chernobyl: New disease, most children sick in area of Belarus." March 31, DOE Watch@topica.com.

Lester, Will. 2005. "Americans" nuclear fears remain: Most say no one should have nukes. *Arizona Republic*, March 31, p. A7.

Maugh II, Thomas H. 2005. "Threshold notion rejected." *Arizona Republic*, June 30, p. A7.

McCord, J. M. 2005. "Uranium mines go back underground." *High Country News*, June 13, p. 5.

Montague, Peter. 2004. "Fiery hell on earth, Part 5: A marriage made in heaven." *Rachel's Environmental & Health News*, #796, July 26, p. 1, http://rachel.org

Munger, Frank. 2005. "Coalition: New rules harm nuke workers." June 5, Munger@knowes.com.

New Yorker. 2010. "The nuclear option." Letter to the Editor, September 27.

Newsweek. 2011. March 28 and April 4, p. 4.

Ozawa, Eric. 2012. "The Fukushima resistance." *Nation*, March 26, 2012, pp. 7-8.

Paskus, Laura. 2005. "Navahos put more than 17 million acres off-limits." *High Country News*, June 13, p. 5.

Pasqualetti, Martin J. (Ed.) 1990. *Nuclear Decommissioning and Society*, New York: Routledge.

Piño, Manny. 1995. "Uranium mining." Interview on June 4 at Arizona State University.

Randazzo, Ryan. 2010. "Cost an obstacle to building reactors." *Arizona Republic*, February 2, pp. B6-B7.

Reader, Mark. 1980. *Atom's Eve: Ending the Nuclear Age.* New York: McGraw-Hill, pp. 116-119.

Riyadi, Slamet. 2010. "Iran begins loading fuel rods." *Arizona Republic*, October 27, p. A3.

Robinson, Eugene. 2011. "Japan disaster underlines dangers of nuclear power." *Arizona Republic*, March 16, p. B5.

Rosner, Hillary. 2005. "Radioactive wasteland cleanup in its last stages." *Arizona Republic*, June 11, p. A27.

Sherman, Janette M. D. 2005. "Cancer tops heart disease as no. 1 killer." *Washington Post*, January 20, p. A12.

Shah, Saeed. 2009. "Terrorist hits near likely nuclear site." *Lexington Herald-Leader*, October 24, p. A9.

Sierra. 2010. "Know you nukes." November/December, p. 45.

Swiss Medical Weekly. 2005. "40% cancer increase in Chernobyl-affected Belarus." March 31, Richard Bramhall, Low Level Radiation Campaign, bramhall@llrc.org.

Vartabedian, Ralph. 2009. "Nevada's hidden ocean of radiation." *New Mexican*, November 14, p. A11.

Wetherbee, G. A., Debey, T. M., Nilles, M. A., Lehmann, C. M. B., and Gay, D. A., 2012. Fission products in National Atmospheric Deposition Program—Wet deposition samples prior to and following the Fukushima Daiichi Nuclear Power Plant incident,

March 8-April 5, 2011: U.S. Geological Survey Open-File Report, 2011—1277, 27 p.

Wiles, Russ. 2011. "Property liability policies don't cover nuclear calamities." *Arizona Republic*, March 27, pp. D1 and D2.

Yablokov, Alexey, Vassily Nesterenko, and Alexey Nesterenko. 2010. *Chernobyl: Consequences of the Catastrophe for People and the Environment*. New York Academy of Sciences.

Yamaguchi, Mari. 2011. "Robots confirm Japan radiation peril." *Arizona Republic*, April 19, p. A3.

Yamaguchi, Mari. 2011. "Reactor's damage is more extensive." *Arizona Republic*, May 13, p. A3.

CHAPTER 2

Environmental Problems in the Nuclear Fuel Cycle: Fernald and Chernobyl

> The greatest minds in the nuclear establishment have been searching for an answer to the radioactive waste problem for fifty years, and they've finally got one; haul it down a dirt road and dump it on an Indian reservation.
>
> —Winona LaDuke, Honor the Earth

Introduction

Deciding on a point of departure for this book was not so simple. There are many ways of focusing on problems within the nuclear fuel cycle, as history demonstrates. For instance, Richard Rhodes (1986) concentrates on the history of the building of the atomic bomb, while Stewart Udall's (1994) work focuses upon deception and personal tragedy surrounding the Cold War itself. Makhijani et al. (1995) provide a "global guide to nuclear weapons production." Bernal et al. (1993) examine childhood cancer rates around nuclear installations. Bertell (1985) and Gofman (1981) are more concerned with the global effects of low-level radiation. Fradkin (1989) is concerned with nuclear fallout from atomic testing in the Nevada desert during the 1950s and 1960s, and Caldicott (2002) reminds us that thousands of nuclear warheads still exist, enough to blow up the world many times over. All these important works should be read carefully by students of atomic history, as well as Soviet works on the same topic.

We decided to focus on the Fernald nuclear weapons plant (technically, "The Feed Materials Production Center") and the disaster at Chernobyl. Although Fernald and Chernobyl are quite different regulatory/institutional "animals" (i.e., civilian power plant vs. weapons plant), what links them is the nuclear fuel cycle (see Figure 1 Nuclear Fuel Cycle). Figure 1 explains how high-level nuclear waste spent fuel can be diverted from storage and used as material for atomic weapons. A single reactor or a few reactors that are carefully controlled are less likely to constitute a serious ecological threat. However, as the volume, frequency, and locations of radioactive transactions increase globally, some are asking how they are going to protect their lives, liberties, and happiness in a world facing nuclear weapons and nuclear electric proliferation, as well as continued mishandling of radioactive materials (Reader et al., 1980: 1 and 5). The nuclear fuel cycle has been called a "death or cancer machine" (Reader et al., 1980: 252) because it manufactures radioactive elements that damage human and other animal cells (Hardert, 1987: 2). In fact, a *rem*, which measures radiation dose, is defined in terms of biological damage to tissue (Geiger et al., 1992: 31).

The primary source of judgments on the effects of low-dose radiation has been the National Academy of Science's succession of expert committees on the Biological Effects of Ionizing Radiation (BEIR), which has periodically reviewed the problem over the past several decades. Each successive revision of the BEIR reports has increased the estimated fatal cancer risks of low-dose radiation.

Thus, along with their linkage to the nuclear fuel cycle, Fernald and Chernobyl have similarities related to nuclear exposure, public health, the risk of accidents, and intergenerational ethics. Chapter 4 on public trust at Fernald and Chapter 5 on nuclear regulatory failure must be understood within the context of these Fernald/ Chernobyl commonalities. If the complexity of the nuclear age seems confusing, we recommend "thinking (nuclear fuel) cycle." For instance, "thinking cycle" puts into context the issues such as "national security" versus "the right to know," and information, or lack thereof, becomes directly related to public trust. The DOE weapons complex (Coyle, 1988) is structured around the (amended) AEA of 1954, which created the classification of nuclear information and generated a national security state of secrecy around plutonium, other fissionable materials, and all atomic energy practices. Hence, it is no accident that a sign placed outside the Fernald weapons plant and pointed in the direction of exiting workers read, "Button Up," that is, keep quiet about your work at the plant. Fernald in Ohio and Chernobyl in the Former Soviet Union became microcosms of the secret, global, nuclear macrocosm.

Thus, by "thinking cycle," we avoid the reductionism of focusing on one facility at a time.

In the next section, we demonstrate the fact that the problems discovered at Fernald/Chernobyl were not atypical within the nuclear weapons and nuclear electric fuel cycles.

Developments within the US Nuclear Weapons Complex

Deadly Defense (edited by Coyle, 1988) provided the first overall view of how the US nuclear weapons production complex is poisoning Americans every day it operates. The book compiles detailed information about the principal bomb production sites and includes a variety of graphics and maps to help make the data more useful to the uninitiated. The irony is that in the name of national security, we have been poisoned by our own government. Indeed, serious radioactive spills have occurred at various points along the US nuclear fuel cycle since March 28, 1979, when the accident at TMI, Unit 2, began, and many more accidents may be anticipated before the fuel cycle is shut down permanently (Reader et al., 1980: 1).

Because the US complex of nuclear production sites is so extensive (i.e., seventeen of them), we decided to focus on only one of them, the less-researched Fernald, along with Chernobyl near Kiev in the Former Soviet Union. The latter plant is included to demonstrate the fact that accidents occur in the nuclear electric cycle as well as in military weapons production. This approach also allows us to view nuclear accidents and "incidents" in an international context, in which various governments have been poisoning their citizens and the global ecosystem.

Although we focus mainly on Fernald and Chernobyl, it seems prudent at the outset to present some developments at other sites in the US weapons fuel cycle as well. Along with the Fernald, there are six other US materials production plants (Mound, Rocky Flats, the Y-12 Plant, Hanford, Savannah River, and Idaho National Engineering Laboratory, INEL). The US complex also includes four research laboratories (Lawrence Livermore National Laboratory, Los Alamos National Laboratory (LANL), Sandia National Laboratories, and Oak Ridge National Laboratory) as well as three gaseous diffusion plants (Portsmouth, Paducah, and Oak Ridge). There is also one testing site (the Nevada Test Site) and a final assembly site (Pantex). The Ashtabula Extrusion Plant of Ohio plays a minor role in nuclear weapons production and is basically an extension of Fernald (Coyle, 1988: 13). Many American cities are unaware of the fact that due to the numerous machine shops and other small "mom-and-pop" facilities that support the total weapons complex, the radiation and chemical cleanup now involves 114 US facilities (*National Geographic*, July 2002: 8).

Secrecy related to nuclear weapons production has resulted in policies and programs "that have torn apart communities and wrecked lives" (Gray, 1995: 8). The absence of public disclosure and oversight has led to some indefensible and dangerous actions and citizen reactions, as the following examples show.

At the Fernald plant in Ohio, a foundry where materials for nuclear weapons were processed released roughly 3 million pounds of toxic uranium dust into the air and water between 1952 and 1989 (McKenna, May 3, 1989). Several local drinking wells were contaminated for years before residents were notified.

The nuclear weapons facilities at Oak Ridge, Tennessee, polluted the environment with about 800,000 pounds of mercury along with numerous other toxic and radioactive materials. Mercury-contaminated soil was used as "fill" at a local church and for a public school playground. Government officials and contractor employees who knew about the contamination were not allowed to alert the public. More recently (Munger, May 11, 2005), an environmental activist group blasted a federal report that said nuclear discharges at Oak Ridge did not pose a public health threat in the past, present, or future. The activist Oak Ridge Environmental Peace Alliance said the federal report's conclusions could not be "supported by science or common sense" and called the report "unconscionable" and "flat-out false." Phelps (May 19, 2005) reports that a local Oak

Ridge doctor, William K. Reid, noted that many of his patients "show signs of heavy metals toxicity."

The Hanford, Washington, site released about 27,000 times as much radioactive iodine-131 into the air as was released by the TMI accident. On at least one occasion, I-131 was emitted deliberately as an experiment. Nearby residents were sometimes exposed to radiation doses hundreds of times the level believed to be safe at the time. Information on these releases was kept secret by the US government from the late 1940s until the mid-1980s.

At LANL, Concerned Citizens for Nuclear Safety (2003) found that emissions of plutonium into the air may be as many as twenty times greater than previously estimated. The report also found increased incidence of breast cancer, melanoma, non-Hodgkin's lymphoma, and ovarian, prostate, testicular, and thyroid cancers in Los Alamos County. Further, the report found that occupational health studies at LANL "have been discriminatory and incomplete." Soon after these revelations, nuclear watchdog groups reported (Tollefson, 2003) finding trace levels of radioactivity in a spring below White Rock, which could mean that groundwater contamination due to nuclear work at LANL is entering the Rio Grande River.

Meanwhile, at Rocky Flats, the DOE plans to let visitors roam 16 miles of trails across a scenic plateau that once housed the Rocky Flats nuclear weapons plant (Elliott, 2004). A Colorado state health official said the 6,240 acres site will be safe for public use after a $7 billion cleanup of plutonium, but some activists disagree. For instance, Le Roy Moore of the Rocky Mountain Peace and Justice Center said, "It's really unwise to allow public recreation on a site that's still contaminated with some levels of plutonium and toxic materials." Newly retired FBI agent Jon Lipsky has presented long-secret evidence of dumping and burning of radioactive waste at Rocky Flats, which he said prosecutors stopped him from pursuing a dozen years ago (Imse, 2005). In 1989, Lipsky led an FBI raid on Rocky Flats, searching for the evidence of environmental crimes. That investigation ended with a 1992 plea bargain that grand jurors in the case consider a "slap on the wrist" (Imse, 2005). Lipsky says he took early retirement specifically to speak out after 12 years of being muzzled because he does not want children to be playing in radioactive dust when the site is opened for hiking, biking, and horseback riding.

At Yucca Mountain, a proposed high-level nuclear waste repository in Nevada, e-mails by several government scientists suggest workers were planning to fabricate records and to manipulate results to ensure outcomes that would help the Yucca Mountain Project move forward (Werner, 2005). Until recently, Yucca Mountain, approved by Congress in 2002, was planned as America's underground repository for 77,000 metric tons of military waste and used reactor fuel from commercial power plants. "But many Nevadans and some environmentalists say the waste can never be safely stored, and the plan puts local residents at risk" (Werner, 2005).

In the nuclear electric area, the award-winning documentary *Three Mile Island Revisited* was aired on Free Speech TV (Dish Network, Channel 9415) at the week of March 28, 2005, the twenty-sixth anniversary of the most serious nuclear plant accident in the US history. This documentary challenges claims of the nuclear industry and US government that "no one died" as a result of the partial core meltdown at Unit 1 of the TMI commercial nuclear complex in Pennsylvania. In fact, the owners of the facility have quietly given cash settlements of up to $1 million to the families of victims. The radioactivity released immediately and for days and weeks afterwards had major health impacts on populations living northeast of TMI. Among those interviewed in *Three Mile Island Revisited* was Debbie Baker, who was pregnant at the time of the accident and whose son was born with Down's Syndrome. She received $1 million and says in the documentary, "I learned that our government covers up many, many things."

Another source (*People*, Summer 2009: 116-117) supports Ms. Baker's claim regarding TMI cover-ups. At first, Metropolitan Edison said that a pump had failed in Unit 2, but that the problem wasn't serious. Then, MetEd admitted, "a small amount" of radioactive water had leaked into the reactor building. Quickly, the estimate of the leak jumped to 50,000 and then to 250,000 gallons. MetEd's president admitted that some radioactive gases had leaked into the atmosphere. When asked how much, he replied, "I'll be honest. I don't know." The electric company initially estimated that less than

1 percent of the plant's fuel rods had been damaged. By week's end, the NRC increased that estimate to 60 percent, the equivalent of a partial core meltdown. In the end, the core temperature of Unit 2 was reduced to a safe level, but nuclear energy itself suffered a *debilitating* blow.

We turn now to a more detailed analysis of one plant in the US nuclear weapons complex, Fernald or the "Feed Materials Production Center" near Ross, Ohio.

Background on Fernald

The Fernald Environmental Management Project, formerly the Feed Materials Production Center, is a 1,050-acre complex located about 17 miles northwest of downtown Cincinnati, Ohio. The facility is owned by the US DOE, and the site was added to the USEPA's Superfund in 1989. Remediation has been ongoing at the site since 1991. From 1952 until 1989, nine plants on the Fernald site processed a wide variety of uranium-containing materials and produced large quantities of radioactive and other toxic wastes. Some wastes were dumped into pits or scrap piles or stored in drums and silos. Production at Fernald ended in July 1989. The most dangerous emissions from Fernald historically have been the radon 222 and radium 226 from "K-65" silos number 1 and 2. Silo 3 also contained radium-bearing wastes, although at lower concentrations (Makhijani and Fioravanti, 1999: 10).

In the fall of 1984, the Feed Materials Production Center near Fernald, Ohio, was identified as the source of uranium contamination for three private wells south of the plant. The author of this book was born and raised in nearby Cincinnati, and his parents, grandparents and an uncle lived within 7 miles of the plant. Thus, he became interested in the reported problem. Eventually, the Fernald situation became his sabbatical leave research project, beginning in 1989 and continuing to the present.

Also in 1984, Charles Zinser rented a vegetable garden near the plant, in order to raise organic vegetables. He often took his two young sons along with him as he worked in this rural setting away from urban Cincinnati's noise and pollution (Magnuson, 1988: 60-65). There was no apparent reason to fear Fernald for, like most Cincinnatians, the Zinsers thought the deceptively named "Feed Materials Production Center" produced food for pets or farm animals. Milk cows grazed along a creek named Paddy's Run, which ran north and south through the Fernald property within the plant's surrounding fences. Equally deceptive for some citizens was a sign in front of the plant with Purina-like checkerboard squares in opposite comers, along with Fernald's typical World War II's water towers, the tops of which were painted in the military's traditional red-and-white checkerboard pattern.

Dairy cows graze in radioactive Paddy's Run.

In April 1986, the Zinsers' oldest son, Sam, was diagnosed with leukemia. Less than 2 months later, in May 1986, the Zinsers' younger son, Louis, followed with a bone tumor in his lower left leg (Magnuson, 1988). At age two, Louis lost the leg, and since there was no apparent cancer history in the family, doctors advised seeking an environmental cause. Subsequently, Charles Zinser had his garden soil tested, and the samples showed higher than normal levels of both uranium-238 and enriched uranium-235. Further, when the Zinsers sent Louis's amputated leg to the University of Waterloo for analysis, the test showed ten times more uranium in the leg than would be expected to accumulate naturally in the lifetime of an adult (Zinser, 1988). Zinser explained, "The doctor said Louis could have eaten dirt and not got that much . . . He said the only way he could have got that much would have been to breathe it" (Magnuson, 1988). Officials from the DOE and Westinghouse Materials Company of Ohio refused to speak with the Zinsers about their son's health problems. Eventually, the Zinsers moved out of Cincinnati to escape unwanted notoriety and criticism from Fernald supporters.

The Feed Materials Production Center, which employed about 1,200 workers at its peak, was an important link in the DOE's chain of seventeen plants that comprised the US nuclear weapons production system. Westinghouse and later contractors, such as Fluor, ran the Fernald cleanup for the DOE after January 1986. But before that, from 1951 through 1985, it was run by NLO, incorporated, a subsidiary of National Lead. Fernald is called a "feed materials center" because it processed various uranium compounds into uranium metal, which it then "fed" to the rest of the US nuclear weapons complex (Coyle, 1988). The uranium metals created at the foundry within Fernald were then used as nuclear weapons parts and in the development of fuel rods for military reactors. Along with the production area, there was a waste storage area that consisted of six waste pits, two concrete waste silos, eighty thousand steel drums, a greenhouse, piles of coal ash, and a 6,500-ton mound of contaminated scrap metal.

Also at Fernald (Coyle, 1988), "the waste pits or settling ponds contain, in addition to more than 11 million pounds of uranium, a toxic soup of other radioactive substances" generated during 38 years of uranium processing. The two "K-65" silos contained radioactive waste from the Manhattan Project, which had leaked out earlier from temporary covers in the form of cancer-causing radon gas (McKenna, June 5, 1990). There were thousands of barrels of radioactive and hazardous chemical wastes stocked outdoors, and numerous barrels of radioactive thorium stored indoors (Higginbotham, August 30, 1990). In terms of volume alone, Fernald is the third largest radioactive waste dump in the United States, behind only Hanford in Richland, Washington, and the Savannah River plant near Aiken, South Carolina. By 1986, Fernald's "realm of waste" had grown to more than 1.1 billion pounds of radioactive and chemical materials (Brataas, October 19, 1986).

By summer 1990, very little, if any, of this waste had been moved off-site (Ullrich, 1990). And by summer 2003, there was still much cleanup left to do (FRESH News, Summer 2003).

Uranium oxide dust emissions into the air and groundwater near Fernald have been a consistent bone of contention between the plant's managers and their critics (McKenna, December 31, 1988). Estimates of emissions into the air during the plant's 38 years of operation reportedly escalated from 200,000 pounds in 1984 to 550,000 pounds by April 1989 (McKenna, May 3, 1989). Based on soil samples and the plant's own production data, at least 600,000 pounds and perhaps as much as 3.08 million pounds (i.e., 1,540 tons) of uranium dust have contaminated the area around the plant—and those estimates could go higher (McKenna, May 3, 1989). The soil samples and computer modeling show that the topsoil within 5 miles of Fernald is covered with 22-1,100 pounds of uranium per square mile (Willette and McKenna, May 4, 1989). Even more unsettling is a plant memo, which says that a mill within the Fernald uranium foundry "leaked so much radioactive thorium that workers used a *bucket* to collect the dust" (Willette and McKenna, May 4, 1989). Thorium-230, as an example, has a radioactive half-life of 180,000 years, which means its daughter products will remain active pollutants for hundreds of years (Winchester, 1979).

Similar revelations have been made regarding Fernald's emissions into groundwater near the plant. All the plant's waste sat atop the Great Miami River Aquifer, a major drinking water resource about 20 miles northwest of downtown Cincinnati. Large amounts of radioactivity from runoff and from the waste pits combined to contaminate the aquifer. Filtrate from the pits combined with other effluents and storm sewer water was released into Paddy's Run creek and areas under the plant. On May 16 and 17, 1990, more than 600,000 gallons of water overflowed a storm-water runoff basin and ran through Paddy's Run—an area previously blamed for allowing uranium to seep through to underlying groundwater supplies. Regarding the latter runoff, the DOE's site environmental manager said that the water contained about 3 pounds of uranium, giving it a concentration of 500-600 parts of uranium per billion parts of water (McKenna, May 23, 1990). The proposed federal drinking-water standard for uranium is no more than 30 parts per billion, and the radioactive half-life of uranium-234 is 250,000 years (Bertell, 1985: 34). Thus, uranium is a highly dangerous radionuclide, as discussed in Chapter 5 of *Deadly Defense* (Coyle, 1988: 115-120).

As mentioned earlier, the DOE had known since late 1984 that the three private wells that drew on the aquifer south of Fernald were contaminated with uranium (McKenna, May 16, 1989). Some readings in those wells were 250 times greater than the maximum levels set by the Environmental Protection Agency (EPA) (Coyle, 1988). Bone and bone marrow radiation doses to people drinking this water were unacceptably high, and the wells were closed (Coyle, 1988). Since then, the DOE has been sinking test wells throughout the area and has discovered plumes of uranium moving south along Paddy's Run (McKenna, May 16, 1989) and in the Great Miami River Aquifer (McKenna, October 25, 1990). According to plant consultants and environmental agencies, about 115 of the 180 test wells drilled after the summer of 1989 revealed contaminated water, with uranium being found less than 20 feet beneath the surface under much of the Fernald plant (McKenna, October 25, 1990). Environmental officials feared this contamination could pose a threat to the entire aquifer because the majority of the test wells were contaminated with uranium to some degree, including levels reaching as high as 10,000 parts per billion in six wells and 1,000 parts per billion in nine other wells (McKenna, October 25, 1990). The highest readings, however, were reported on February 8, 1990, when samples taken from beneath the plant held 696,000 parts of uranium per billion parts of water (McKenna, February 8, 1990). Another "water pocket" discovered 20 feet below the plant's refinery showed contamination of 28,000-40,000 parts per billion. More troublesome is the fact that it took until August 1990 for the DOE to publicly admit that cesium-137 had been released into Paddy's Run and that thorium-230 had been found in soil samples around the Fernald site (Higginbotham, August 30, 1990).

After extensive review of government documents, the Radioactive Waste Campaign (Coyle, 1988) found the six Fernald waste pits to be the primary cause of groundwater contamination at the plant. The pits were not isolated from the groundwater system, and some pits were actually being fed by springs. The campaign contends that recent construction at Fernald will, at best, transplant some radiation from the private drinking wells into the Great Miami River and to a larger downstream population while leaving the heart of the contamination problems—the six waste pits—untouched (Coyle, 1988). Part of the waste problem at Fernald is the relatively small facility site, only 1,050 acres compared with Hanford's 570 square miles, and the fact that more than a million people live within a 20-mile radius of the plant. Ironically, in early 1951, the old AEC—predecessor to the present DOE—was warned by the US Geological Survey that due to the hydrogeology of the area, groundwater contamination could occur at Fernald if the wastes "were not handled carefully" (Peck, March 18, 1987).

Regarding potential health problems at Ohio's Fernald plant, Marvin Resnikoff, coauthor of *Deadly Defense,* (1988) predicted an additional 185 cancers in the neighborhoods around the plant due to residents' exposure to the various types of radiation mentioned earlier (Neus, February 5, 1990). Dr. Alice Stewart, a British epidemiologist and leading authority on the effects of radiation on humans, thinks that people living close to Fernald "have suffered worse than those at TMI" (McKenna and Neus, April 28, 1989). This hypothesis relates to the fact that Fernald contaminated the environment with low-level radiation for 38 years, while TMI was one large, but short-lived, accident. The DOE's long-promised release of the health and work records of 300,000 past and present employees at Fernald and nuclear arms plants elsewhere might unravel some of the mystery. But this assumes a number of things: that the DOE data will be released in a form that can be analyzed by independent researchers, that is, complete with some type of worker *identifiers*; that the data on worker radiation exposures are fundamentally correct, as monitored by film badges worn by plant personnel; and that long-term, independent research funding can be assured, especially given the methodological complexities involved in this type of research (McKenna, January 18, 1990).

Meanwhile, it took the DOE nearly 6 years (fall 1984 until spring 1990) to agree to fund most of the cleanup at Fernald (McKenna, April 10, 1990). And within the total projected cleanup cost of $227 billion for all seventeen US weapons production plants (Makhijani and Fioravanti, 1999), it is worth noting that Fernald was projected as a top recipient of money for cleanup (Willette, January 16, 1990). The DOE's 5-year plan for cleanup earmarked $656 million to treat radioactive and chemical wastes in the drums, pits, and silos at the Feed Materials Production Center. That amount is second only to $964 million then projected for the Hanford Reservation, by some accounts the most polluted and dangerous site in the US nuclear weapons complex.

Some progress has been made in the cleanup at Fernald. According to Lisa Crawford (FRESH News, Summer 2003), president of FRESH, more contaminated buildings came down, an on-site disposal facility "has grown by leaps and bounds, roads have been closed, acres of land have been cleared and cleaned up, waste pits are becoming huge holes in the ground, and the silos have so much construction around them you can hardly see them from the road." Further, as of June 2003, Fluor Fernald Corporation decontaminated and dismantled 124 of the 223 structures that needed to be taken down at the site. This was good news given the billions of taxpayers' dollars that have been spent and the fact that FRESH has been working on this environmental issue for over 23 years.

Cost estimates for total environmental management activities at the Fernald site reached $5.4 billion in 1999 and monitoring *activities* there could stretch to the year 2030 (Makhijani and Fioravanti, 1999: 1).

More than the economic cost of the nuclear age, however, it is the human cost that troubles many scientists and environmentalists, as reflected in the experience of the Zinser family and many others who trusted the government. As Alice Stewart expressed it, "At the end of every statistic is a person, and something that happened to that person" (McKenna and Neus, April 28, 1989). It remains to be seen whether or not a groundswell of moral indignation will develop against these plants and if that public opinion will be enough to close down the nuclear weapons industry permanently. However, it must be kept in mind that former President George W. Bush initiated a "second nuclear age," ordering up a new generation of small atomic bombs, which are deemed to be needed because they are "more usable" than older, larger A-bombs. Mr. Bush also announced provocative new war policies, including the threat of preemptive nuclear strikes against America's enemies, even enemies without nuclear arms (Montague, 2004: 1).

A thumbnail sketch of other plants in the US weapons chain indicates that Fernald may be only the tip of the iceberg. Similar environmental conditions exist at all seventeen nuclear weapons facilities, but several situations deserve special mention (Coyle, 1988). At the Hanford Reservation in Washington State, billions of gallons of contaminated water were poured into seepage beds, resulting in a surface plume of radioactive tritium that has moved 6 miles to the Columbia River and has contaminated a deep underground aquifer with radioactive iodine-129. The Public Broadcasting System (1990) reported that so much radiation leaked onto the Hanford site that even the local rabbits and their feces were radioactive. Even more incredible was *Time* (Magnuson, 1988) magazine's revelation that

> "At the sprawling Hanford plutonium-processing complex in Washington State, managers once deliberately released 5,050 curies of radioactive iodine into the air. The reason: to see if they could reduce the amount of time uranium must be cooled before being processed into plutonium, presumably to increase production."

Perhaps the fact that the DOE has finally officially admitted the releases noted above may serve as a kind of vindication for those among the 270,000 exposed persons who later developed thyroid cancer (Schumacher, July 24, 1990).

Another nuclear weapons facility that deserves public scrutiny is Rocky Flats near Denver. At risk are populations that use water from Broomfield Great Western Reservoir and Standley Lake, both of which have been polluted by plutonium-239 (radioactive half-life = 24,400 years) from the Rocky Flats plant. Storms and other natural occurrences could stir up the radioactive sediments and expose people using these water sources to increased radioactivity. In the early 1970s, Dr. Carl Johnson, former director of the Jefferson County Board of Health, documented elevated cancer rates for male and female residents living in neighborhoods near Rocky Flats (Johnson, 1984). And medical records of fourteen Rocky Flats plant employees who have contracted cancer indicate there is a "consistent pattern of exposure to radioactive materials" (*Cincinnati Enquirer*, November 19, 1989). A third study of Rocky Flats found the death rate from brain tumors among white male workers to be twice that of a similar group not exposed to radiation (Cobb, 1989).

The Savannah River plant also has large quantities of nuclear waste stored in landfills, seepage basins, and fifty-one underground storage tanks (Malloy, 1990). About 30 million gallons of radioactive effluent were discharged annually into the basins. From 1953 to 1978, 2.5 billion gallons of contaminated liquids were discharged, and through 1976, over 500,000 curies of tritium were released to seepage basins. Substantial leaching of burial grounds and surface impoundments is causing severe contamination of surface water and groundwater, thus endangering the Tuscaloosa aquifer used by Atlanta.

Finally, between 1952 and 1970, the INEL near Idaho Falls dumped 16 billion gallons of wastewater containing 70,000 curies of radioactivity into the Snake River Plain Aquifer via deep injection wells on their premises (Malloy, 1990). As a result of this waste disposal, the aquifer contains plutonium, strontium-90, cesium, cobalt-60, tritium, and iodine-129 (Malloy, 1990). Boise State University sociology Professor Michael Blain studied the health impact of INEL on residents of Clark County near the site and contends that cancer deaths and breast malignancies there have occurred at about twice the normal rate (Magnuson, 1988).

Thus, the production of seventy thousand nuclear weapons over more than 60 years in the United States has created volumes of long-lived radioactive waste, decommissioning problems related to thousands of nuclear facilities, and environmental concerns involving contaminated land and water. The DOE is responsible for managing some 36 million cubic meters of radioactive and other hazardous wastes in a wide array of forms and storage configurations at 137 sites (Makhijani and Fioravanti, 1999: 1).

The US nuclear weapons production and related activities have contaminated 79 million cubic meters of soil and almost 2 billion cubic meters of groundwater. Additionally, the DOE manages an estimated 820,000 metric tons of "miscellaneous" materials, including 585,000 metric tons of depleted uranium, mostly in the form of uranium hexafluoride (Makhijani and Fioravanti, 1991: 1). Workers at the Fernald uranium foundry in Ohio converted hundreds of tons of uranium hexafluoride gas into "green-salt" crystals. These crystals were blended with magnesium granules in a furnace. The cooked mixture unites, converting the green-salt crystals into uranium metal. Some of this metal was made into reactor fuel for plutonium production at the Hanford and Savannah River production plants (U.S. Department of Energy Office of Environmental Management, 1995: 15).

Regarding health effects near the Fernald plant, in March 1998, the Centers for Disease Control (CDC) provided the results of the first phase of the "Fernald Risk Assessment Project." Lung cancer was the most likely health outcome associated with radionuclides (primarily radon and uranium) released to the environment during Fernald operations from 1951 through 1988. The results outlined in the CDC report include estimates of the number of lung cancer deaths occurring in the community from 1951 through 2088 that may be due to exposure to radioactive materials released from Fernald during its production years. The CDC also projected estimates of the percentage increase in the number of lung cancer deaths over the number that would be expected in the absence of those exposures.

While the CDC (March 1988) could not actually identify specific lung cancer deaths caused by Fernald exposure, they estimated that the number of lung cancer deaths occurring between 1952 and 2088 may be increased by 1-12 percent as a result of Fernald-related radiation exposures. The CDC further predicted that about half the number of lung cancer deaths potentially related to Fernald radiation exposure occurred through the period ending in the year 2000, while the other half was predicted to occur in the time period from 2001 to 2088.

Finally, the 1998 CDC results indicate that the estimated percentage increase in the number of Fernald-related lung cancer deaths that may have occurred *before* the year 2000 is about three times the value predicted for the later time period (2001-2088). This is because the study population is aging and their background rates of lung cancer mortality and mortality due to causes other than lung cancer are increasing as they age.

In terms of health, the above findings may represent only the tip of the iceberg since 3,700 toxic waste sites also have been located on regular military installations of our air force, army, and navy (Public Broadcasting System, 1988).

The Soviet Nuclear Waste Legacy

Nuclear weapons production has been veiled in secrecy globally since its inception more than 65 years ago. Specific examples (summarized from U.S. Department of Energy Office of Environmental Management, 1995: 77) can provide perspective on the environmental legacy of nuclear weapons production in the Former Soviet Union.

Techa River Contamination

The Techa River flows past the Mayak plutonium-production complex in the Southern Ural Mountains in the Chelyabinsk region of Central Russia. From 1949 until 1951, the Soviets pumped 2.6 billion cubic feet of liquid, high-level radioactive waste directly into the Techa River. Without telling the residents why, Soviet authorities evacuated about eight thousand people from twenty villages. A 1992 photo (U.S. Department of Energy Office of Environmental Management, 1995: 76) depicts concerned women from the village of Muslyimovo in the Southern Urals standing on the banks of the Techa and watching a group of Westerners taking radiation readings.

Radiation levels today in this area are thirty to sixty times higher than natural background radiation.

The job of Chelyabinsk-65 and its five atomic reactors was to enrich uranium and plutonium to bomb-grade purity. When a surfeit of this material was reached in 1990, the last of the reactors was shut down. But not before 1.2 billion curies of long-lasting radiation was unleashed on the region.

Dr. Elena Zhukovskaya, a cancer expert at Chelyabinsk Region Children's Hospital, treated more than three hundred children from that region who were suffering from leukemia. She found that the rate of leukemia was 33 percent higher than normal among children from Chelyabinsk-65 and two other closed "nuclear cities" in the area (Witt, 1992: 5). When compared to the leukemia rate in other areas that were heavily polluted with industrial wastes, but *not* radiation, the Chelyabinsk area still scored twice as high. "Undoubtedly, the leukemia problem is related to radiation," Zhukovskaya said (Witt, 1992: 5).

Lake Karachai

The contamination of the Techa River ended the practice of dumping high-level nuclear waste directly into the river. But from 1948 until the late 1950s, engineers at the Mayak dumped high-level waste directly into a small lake called Lake Karachai instead. Some 120 million curies of high-level waste, equal to about one-eighth of all the high-level waste generated within the US nuclear complex, remains in Lake Karachai today. Workers filling in some of the reservoirs of Lake Karachai with concrete and dirt had to operate their machines from radiation-shielded cabs. Thus, a person standing at some points on the lake's shore would receive a fatal dose of radiation in less than an hour (Witt, 1992: 5). In times of drought, severely contaminated sediment from the lake's bottom dried out and was dispersed over 1,000 square miles by the wind. The first such episode convinced the Soviets that this situation was unwise, so they began storing their radioactive waste in above-ground tanks. "This is our reality. Things were done in a terrible haste and in complete ignorance of the principles of running such an industry," said Yevgeny Ryzhkov, the manager of public communications at Chelyabinsk-65 (Witt, 1992: 5). "We made tragic mistakes, like the decision to dump wastes into the Techa. But it was not a deliberate decision to expose people. They just did not think about the consequences, and they didn't know all the dangers."

Mayak Waste—Tank Explosion

In 1957, an 80,000-gallon tank of high-level waste at Mayak exploded with a force of 5-10 tons of dynamite, heavily contaminating about 9,000 square miles of Soviet land. The average radiation dose received by ten thousand people evacuated from the region was about 50 rem or ten times the 1995 annual limit for the US workers. This accident was kept secret by Soviet officials until 1980. Some 75 square miles remain uninhabitable today.

Waste Pumped Underground

As a result of the problems experienced at Mayak, other Soviet weapons production sites began to pump high-level waste deep underground into rock formations that they believed would keep the waste from spreading and reaching the human environment. The quantity of the waste thus disposed of was large (i.e., about 1.5 billion curies), and most of the pumping occurred at the Siberian plutonium production sites—Tomsk-7 on the Tom River and Krasnoyarsk-26 on the Yenisey River. The Soviets dumped other radioactive liquids into rivers and reservoirs near these sites.

The Arctic Ocean

Today, the Tom and Yenisey Rivers in Siberia are contaminated for hundreds of miles downstream. Some of the radioactive waste that was released into these rivers has ended up in the Arctic Ocean, where it has entered the ecosystem and endangered fisheries. Over the years, the Soviet navy dumped fifteen nuclear submarine reactors and other highly radioactive materials directly into the Arctic Ocean. They also dumped radioactive waste into countless rivers and lakes. Fallout from nuclear weapons testing on the arctic island of Novaya Zemlya has also contributed to the contamination of the Siberian arctic.

New Attitudes

During the Cold War, the US national security strategy was based on deterring a large-scale Soviet attack by maintaining a large nuclear arsenal. The Soviets viewed America in much the same way. Now, the definition of "national security" is expanding to include other concerns, such as the environment, the human health, the global economy, the terrorism, and the spread of nuclear weapons.

Understanding these new goals, countries are sharing information and opening up their once-secret facilities. It is hoped that through such sharing, scientists, engineers, and policymakers can build trust, reduce health, environmental, and safety risks, and decrease the threat of nuclear weapons proliferation. Such alliances could form the basis for new world security.

The dismantling of surplus weapons and production plants can also increase trust between the United States and its former Cold War adversaries (*McClatchy Newspapers*, 2010: 9). Surplus plutonium and highly enriched uranium in the United States and Russia are being opened up to international monitoring. For instance, representatives of the IAEA and the Russian government have already toured key US production facilities at Hanford, Rocky Flats, and Oak Ridge. In addition, joint projects with Russia are helping the Russian government ensure that crucial materials for nuclear weapons are accounted for and well-guarded. In 1991, the United States began a program to assist the Russians in dismantling their nuclear weapons and in managing their stockpiles of plutonium and highly enriched uranium as safely and securely as possible. The DOE (USDOE) has also played a key role in efforts to secure weapons-grade nuclear materials globally. The DOE's Reduced Enrichment Research and Test Reactor program is aimed at eliminating international commerce in highly enriched uranium fuel for reactors—a material that could be diverted and used to make nuclear weapons.

The plan for the rest of the book is to continue to deal with Fernald and to analyze similar issues surrounding Chernobyl in Chapters 4 and 5.

References

Bernal, V., E. Roman, and M. Bobrow. 1993. *Childhood Cancer and Nuclear Installations*. London: BMJ.

Bertell, R. 1985. *No Immediate Danger*. Summertown, TN: The Book Publishing Company, p. 34.

Brataas, A. 1986. "Pit liner failed twice." *Cincinnati Enquirer*. October 19, pp. A-1 and ff.

Caldicott, H. 2002. *The New Nuclear Danger*. NY: The New Press.

Centers for Disease Control and Prevention. 1998. "A Summary of the Draft Fernald Risk Assessment Report: Estimation of the Impact of the Former Feed Materials Production Center (FMPC) on Lung Cancer Mortality in the Surrounding Community." March.

Cincinnati Enquirer. 1989. "Radiation exposure claimed." November 19.

Cobb, C. E. 1989. "Living with radiation." *National Geographic*. June, pp. 403-437.

Concerned Citizens for Nuclear Safety. 2003. "Right to know." *New Mexican*. September 22.

Coyle, D. 1988. *Deadly Defense: Military Radioactive Landfills*. New York: Radioactive Waste Campaign, pp. 115-120.

Elliott, D. 2004. "Trails at ex-nuclear plant." *Arizona Republic*. December 18, p. A35.

Fradkin, P. L. 1989. *Fallout: An American Nuclear Tragedy*. Tucson: University of Arizona Press.

FRESH News. Summer 2003. Vol. 33: 1-8. FRESH, Inc., P. O. Box 129, Ross, OH 45061-0129.

Geiger, H. J., D. Rush, et al. 1992. *Deadly Reckoning*. Washington: Physicians for Social Responsibility.

Gofman, J. 1981. *Radiation & Human Health*. San Francisco: Sierra Club Books.

Gray, P. 1995. *Facing Reality: Ending the Culture of Secrecy in the U.S. Nuclear Weapons Complex*. San Francisco: The Tides Foundation.

Hardert, R. 1987. "Nuclear children: Health consequences of the nuclear fuel and weapons cycles." *Research in Contemporary and Applied Geography*. Vol. 11, No. 4, pp. 1-6.

Higginbotham, M. 1990. "Reports reveal more hazards at Fernald." *Cincinnati Enquirer*, August 30, p. C-2.

Imse, A. 2005. "Ex-agent outlines Flats allegations." *Rocky Mountain News*, January 6.

Johnson, C. 1984. "Cancer incidence in an area of radioactive fallout downwind from the Nevada Test Site." *Journal of the American Medical Association*, Vol. 251, pp. 230-236.

Makhijani, A., and M. Fioravanti. 1999. "Cleaning up the cold war mess." *Science for Democratic Action*. January, Vol. 7, No. 2, pp. 1-23.

Makhijani, A., H. Hu, and K. Yih. 1995. *Nuclear Wastelands.* Cambridge, MA: MIT Press.

Magnuson, E. 1988. "They lied to us." *Time.* October 31, pp. 60-65.

Malloy, P. J. 1990. "Newsletter." Radioactive Waste Campaign, January 3.

McClatchy Newspapers. 2010. "U.S. helps Kazakhstan move nuclear materials." November 17, p. A9.

McKenna, M. A. J. 1990. "Fernald exposure data called defective." *Cincinnati Enquirer,* January 18, pp. A-1 and ff.

McKenna, M. A. J. 1990. "New water threat at Fernald." *Cincinnati Enquirer,* February 8, pp. A-1 and ff.

McKenna, M. A. J. 1990. "Fernald cleanup set to begin." *Cincinnati Enquirer,* April 10, p. A-1.

McKenna, M. A. J. 1990. "Tainted water overflowed near Fernald." *Cincinnati Enquirer.* May 23, pp. E-1 and E-2.

McKenna, M. A. J. 1990. "Twister could have spread Fernald radiation." *Cincinnati Enquirer,* June 5, p. A-6.

McKenna, M. A. J. 1990. "Fernald may be threat to aquifer." *Cincinnati Enquirer.* October 25, pp. E-1 and E-2.

McKenna, M. A. J., and E. Neus. 1989. "Worse than Three Mile Island." *Cincinnati Enquirer.* April 28, pp. C-1 and C-2.

McKenna, M. A. J. 1989. "Uranium found in soil." *The Cincinnati Enquirer.* May 16, pp. A-1 and A-12.

McKenna, M. A. J. 1989. "Estimates soar for radiation lost at Fernald." *Cincinnati Enquirer.* May 3, pp. A-1 and ff.

McKenna, M. A. J. 1988. "Memo raises Fernald figures." *Cincinnati Enquirer.* December 31, pp. A-1 and ff.

Montague, Peter. "God told me to strike." Fiery Hell on Earth, Part 4. Rachel's Environment and Health News #795: 1-10. July 8, 2004.

Munger, F. 2005. "Alliance slams nuke report." May 11. Mungerffinews.com

National Geographic. 2002 (July). "Half life." p. 8.

Neus, E. 1990. "Nuclear arms plants topic of 3 speakers." *Cincinnati Enquirer.* February 5.

Peck, L. 1987. "Agency reported on potential Fernald danger in 1951." Gannett News Service reported in *Cincinnati Enquirer,* March 18.

Phelps, J. 2005. "Comments on April 25, 05 draft for White Oak and ORR releases." May 19. <magnu 96196@aol.com>.

People (magazine). 2009. "Celebrate the 70s!" Summer, pp. 116-117.

Public Broadcasting System. 1990. "The Bomb's lethal legacy." Aired in Phoenix, Arizona, on September 11.

Public Broadcasting System. 1988. "Poison and the Pentagon." Aired in Phoenix, Arizona, by KAET-TV.

Reader, M., R. Hardert, and G. Moulton. 1980. *Atom's Eve: Ending the Nuclear Age.* NY: McGraw-Hill.

Rhodes, R. 1986. *The Making of the Atomic Bomb.* New York: Simon & Schuster.

Schumacher, E. 1990. "Radiation report is vindication." *Seattle Times,* July 24.

Tollefson, J. 2003. "Groups detect cesium in area spring." *New Mexican,* October 27.

Udall, S. 1994. *The Myths of August.* New York: Pantheon.

Ullrich, D. A. 1990. "Statement of David A. Ullrich, Acting Director, Waste Management Division, U.S. Environmental Protection Agency, Region V, Before the Transportation and Hazardous Materials Subcommittee of the House Committee on Energy and Commerce." July 5, pp. 1-5.

U.S. Department of Energy Office of Environmental Management. 1995. "Closing the circle on the splitting of the atom." Office of Strategic Planning and Analysis (EM-4), January.

Werner, E. 2005. "Yucca Mountain e-mails get released." *Arizona Republic,* April 2, p. A15.

Willette, A. 1990. "Fernald's cleanup ranks near top of DOE's budget." Gannett News Service, January 16.

Willette, A., and M. A. J. McKenna. 1989. "Bucket caught Fernald radioactive dust." Gannett News Service and *Cincinnati Enquirer.* May 4, pp. C-1 and C-2.

Winchester, E. 1979. Newsletter. "Nuclear wastes." *Sierra.* July/ August.

Witt, Howard. 1992. "Radioactive river in Russia a deadly legacy of carelessness." *Chicago Tribune,* December 27, pp. 1 and 5.

Zinser, C. 1988. Interview with Charles Zinser on National Public Radio, October 30.

CHAPTER 3

Nuclear Secrecy and Deception
at the Fernald Plant

> All of us who are concerned for peace and triumph
> of reason and justice must be keenly aware how small an
> influence reason and good will exert upon events in the
> political field.

—Albert Einstein

Introduction

The problem we are going to examine in this chapter is the US DOE's Feed Materials Production Center, near Fernald, Ohio. Our purpose is to investigate possible political deception at Fernald, including community reaction to such deception in the form of psychosocial effects, distrust of government, and subsequent litigation. Methods employed in this study include participant observation and interviews with thirty-five families and individuals living within a 7-mile radius of the plant. Other data sources used include: DOE and GAO documents; information supplied by one of the DOE contractors, Westinghouse; hundreds of articles published by the *Cincinnati Enquirer* newspaper; and analysis of the nuclear weapons plant itself. In the Fernald case, the DOE and its subcontractors were slow to announce the discovery of radioactive contamination when it occurred. Observed examples of deception involving public health issues diminished community trust in its formal institutions.

Since the publication of Adeline Gordon Levine's *Love Canal* in 1982, sociologists, politicians, and the public have become increasingly concerned about the inadequacies of hazardous waste management policies, including site selection for the disposal and storage of hazardous waste (Edelstein, 1988; Erikson, 1990; Peck, 1989). This concern includes recent consequences of nuclear waste contamination in various parts of the United States and around the world. It is demonstrated through analyses of risk management and via social activism as in the case of continued organized protest at the nuclear test site, near Mercury, Nevada.

Deciding on a theoretical point of departure for analysis of the Fernald data was not as straightforward as might be expected. One might review the existing literature on state regulation of environmental problems and hypothesize that sociologists, with the possible exception of William Chambliss (1978) and Henry Etzkowitz (1984), have largely failed to recognize the potential of governmental actors to pollute and/or to condone pollution. One might also consult the Marxist literature, which usually assumes that pollution is created by private-sector capitalists. Alternatively, one might examine the growing body of work on trust/trustworthiness by other researchers, for example, Lee Clarke (1989), Jeffrey Ross (2000), Mary Douglas and Aaron Wildovsky (1982), Peter Manning (1988), and Charles Perrow (1984), in order to argue for the importance of case study. We elected the latter approach while retaining an interest in the potential for governmental actors to pollute and/or to excuse pollution, especially within a context of secrecy and deception (Chambliss, 1978: 151) as discussed in Chapter 2.

The proper functioning of society requires that its agencies, particularly those of a scientific and technical kind, demonstrate extremely high performance levels (Perrow, 1984). Similarly, those who care about the credibility of science and technology have a genuine interest in making sure that scientific agencies actually perform their functions responsibly. One of the more-or-less tacit assumptions in the regulation literature is that while the actions of private business may be "problematic," the actions of federal agencies tend to be "unproblematic." Our purpose here is to use a case-study approach in order to determine whether or not this assumption is justified.

We begin with a brief, physical description of the Fernald plant and how it fits into the US nuclear weapons complex. We then provide: a discussion of the theory and method employed in the present study and an analysis of probable deception at Fernald; a comparison between the situation at Fernald and other cases involving possible nuclear deception at the national level; a comparison of the resultant legal problems surrounding both Fernald and Rocky Flats; and a concluding discussion of community response to hazardous waste exposure, including issues of trust, trustworthiness, and the potentially problematic behaviors of government actors.

The DOE Weapons Complex and Fernald

Since the early 1950s, the US DOE has produced the nation's nuclear arsenal at a complex composed of seventeen sites. This complex has come under withering criticism even from official sources, such as the EPA, the GAO, and agents of the DOE itself (see LaGrone, 1989; U.S. Department of Energy, Oak Ridge Operations Office, 1990). All the DOE facilities have been run by private contractors—an arrangement that is officially attributed to the desire for private-sector efficiency but which has increased the potential for mismanagement and environmental contamination. As the power and influence of large corporations has expanded in recent decades, a changing conception of the role and responsibility of these giant organizations has emerged. Widespread reports of corporate misbehavior, ranging from worker exploitation to deception regarding environmental pollution, have made citizens increasingly aware of the costs associated with this type of big business. Consequently, the public is becoming less accepting of corporations' pursuit of profits at any cost and is beginning to require that organizations not only refrain from harming society but also contribute actively to the public good (Crawford, June 2003). The modern view is that social power necessitates social responsibility. Corporations, politicians, and the military are being asked to exercise moral judgment in decision-making—to have a conscience.

Niels Bohr, a Nobel laureate and one of the century's greatest physicists, maintained in 1939 that an atomic bomb could not be built without "turning the country into a gigantic factory" (Rhodes, 1986: 500). Russell (1990: 21) underscores the accuracy of Bohr's prediction, saying:

> "Before nuclear weapons are built, they take shape in the minds and on the drawing boards of scientists at federal laboratories at Los Alamos, New Mexico and Livermore, California. The designs are tested at the Nevada Test Site and the Tonopah Test Range in Nye County, Nevada, then are incorporated into operational weapons systems at Laboratories at Livermore and at Albuquerque, New Mexico. From there, the journey through the sprawling DOE weapons-production system begins."

Russell (1990: 21) provides further detail. The uranium needed to produce the plutonium essential for nuclear weapons was mined in more than one hundred underground and open-pit mines in Wyoming, Colorado, New Mexico, Utah, and Texas. At Fernald, Ohio, enriched uranium was converted to metal for nuclear reactor fuel and shipped to the nearby extrusion plant in Ashtabula, Ohio, where it was shaped into fuel rods. At Hanford and Savannah River, uranium was irradiated in reactors, and some was transformed into plutonium. Rocky Flats manufactured all plutonium parts, as well as other components for nuclear weapons, which were sent to the Pantex Plant in Amarillo, Texas. At Pantex, all pieces came together for final assembly.

Although this above description is greatly oversimplified, it lays the groundwork for understanding how accidents and leaks can and do occur in the nuclear fuel cycle. At Fernald, for example, two concrete (K-65) silos were filled with hundreds of thousands of cubic feet of radioactive wastes from the Manhattan Project, "including radium, radon, uranium, and an undetermined amount of thorium" (LaGrone, 1989: 10). Fernald released more than 3,080,000 pounds of uranium oxide, contaminating surrounding soil and water supplies for miles around and under the plant (Physicians for Social Responsibility, 1989). According to the manager of the US DOE's Oak Ridge operations, "a continuous plume of contamination has been detected approximately 4,100 feet south of the FMPC (Fernald) boundary" and "elevated levels of uranium have also been detected in a monitoring well and a domestic well approximately 2,000 feet due north of the FMPC boundary" (LaGrone, 1989: 25).

Conditions at the other sixteen facilities that, with Fernald, comprise the US nuclear weapons complex are similar (Physicians for Social Responsibility, 1989: 1-2). The Rocky Flats plant, for instance, leaked organic chemicals into groundwater north of Denver, and "the soil around the site is contaminated with plutonium at elevated levels" (Physicians for Social Responsibility, 1989: 2), partly because of a major fire in 1957 at the plutonium-production building "released tens of thousands of millicuries of alpha radiation into the atmosphere." Estimates of released contamination at Rocky Flats are difficult to determine because smokestack monitors and filtration systems were destroyed by explosions and by over two hundred fires at the plant. Following a 1969 fire, measurable amounts of plutonium were found in the soils east of the plant. This could be important history for as Dr. Carl Johnson (1989 speech) points out, "Alpha radiation does not penetrate the skin, but it can be a more damaging type of radiation (than either beta or gamma radiation) if ingested." Further, Dr. Helen Caldicott (1978: 65) explains that plutonium is so toxic that less than one-millionth of a gram is a carcinogenic dose. Plutonium is one of a large number of existing radioactive elements that are toxic. Some other radioactive elements are *more* toxic per unit mass than is plutonium, "but plutonium and its compounds are among the most carcinogenic substances known" (Colorado Council on Rocky Flats, 1993: 19).

In 1987, G. S. Wilkinson conducted a study that addressed plutonium exposure in workers who had died after having worked at Rocky Flats for at least 2 years (Colorado Council on Rocky Flats, 1993: 27). The results of this study showed increased deaths by all causes in employees who carried a plutonium body burden of more than 2 microcuries. Wilkinson also found a greater than expected incidence of brain tumors among Rocky Flats's workers.

In 1989, the FBI raided Rocky Flats after being informed that plant operators were hiding evidence of widespread radioactive contamination (Russell, 1990). They found numerous violations of safety and health regulations (Jakubauskas, 1991). Rockwell

International, the DOE contractor at the time, was terminated and EG&G (Edgerton, Germestausen & Grier) took over. Plutonium production was shut down at the plant, and cleanup operations, similar to those at Fernald, began. Over the years, 62 pounds of plutonium had become trapped in one building's ventilation system alone—enough to fuel seven nuclear bombs (Russell, 1990). As a result of the collapse of the Soviet Union during the fall and winter of 1991-1992, Rocky Flats is no longer assigned an active plutonium-manufacturing mission (Colorado Council on Rocky Flats, 1993). In its 1992 report to Congress, the DOE outlined plans for phasing out both nuclear and nonnuclear production work at the plant and moved into a cleanup mode.

Theory and Method

Earlier success in analyzing development of the nuclear power industry in the United States from a structural point of view (Hardert et al., 1989) motivated returning to critical thinkers, such as Michel Foucault, for help in understanding how deception and secrecy might have been initiated and maintained at Fernald. Foucault (1977) rejects analysis based on abstract, formal theory construction and on hypothesis formation and testing as "devices of domination and control," preferring instead to study the empirical, for example, human interaction, specific historical events, written documents, and the personal power relationships that exist at the *unregulated* margins of the society. Although Foucault's main purpose has been to articulate a loose-knit theory of power, and his major concept has been human subjection (i.e., subjugation), his social structural point of view is unique. In his discussion of "methodological precautions" (Foucault, 1977: 96-102), he says that structural analysis should not concern itself with *legitimate* forms of power (i.e., authority) in central locations but instead must deal with "power at the extreme points of its exercise, where it is always less legal in character." In other words, it may be more important to analyze the actual behaviors of DOE's representatives and operatives, such as Fernald's National Lead and Westinghouse, than to focus on what the DOE says they are doing, have done, will do, or intended to do in the past. Intentions count for very little in Foucault's framework, and power must be studied where it is practiced and produces its real effects.

Foucault's methodology (1977: 96-102) assumes that power must be viewed as something that circulates as a net-like organization, in which individuals simultaneously submit to and exercise power. He claims that individuals are not only power's inert or consenting targets but always the elements of its articulation. He further warns his readers that it is essential to conduct an ascending, empirical analysis of power, starting with the most infinitesimal mechanisms, for it is these that are basic to the more general phenomena. Finally, Foucault says that we should be aware that major mechanisms of power might be accompanied by "ideological productions" that function as effective instruments for the formation and accumulation of knowledge and for what passes as knowledge. In short, we must "base our analysis of power on the study of the techniques and tactics of domination" (Foucault, 1977: 102). This includes an effort to understand how representatives of nuclear elites present themselves to the public.

This approach leads to a question: how do we apply Foucault's theory of power/knowledge to the situation existing at Fernald in order to produce a better understanding of possible deception and how it might function if it did occur? First, Foucault believes that what is available for immediate observation yields only partial knowledge; what is not easily observable or is hidden may be crucial for understanding the problem at hand. Thus, analysis based on formal observation and official data alone, such as an examination of DOE publications or the records of National Lead and Westinghouse at Fernald, would lead to inauthentic or incomplete knowledge.

Second, Foucault further defines his methodology by distinguishing between two types of knowledge: formal knowledge and popular knowledge. *Formal knowledge* is linked with, defines, and is defined by power—for instance, the knowledge of academic disciplines studied in colleges and universities. *Subjugated knowledge* is a form of popular knowledge that is "disguised within the body of functionalist and systematizing theory" (Foucault, 1977: 82). Subjugated knowledge is not a "general common sense knowledge but, on the contrary, a particular, local, regional knowledge capable of unanimity" among observers (Foucault, 1977: 82).

Third, Foucault indicates that a focus on observables alone does not help us understand how certain social problems are generated. As Erving Goffman (1959) and Scott Renshaw (2004) contend, one must get behind or beyond mere appearances (i.e., impression management) in order to gain in-depth understanding of psychosocial problems, particularly those involving secrecy and deception as practiced by various societal elites.

We follow Foucault's methodological precautions, giving consideration to both formal and subjugated knowledge, in order to achieve a better understanding of probable deception at Fernald. Evidence of deception would justify extension of the analysis to other weapons plants in the United States. Following Foucault, "subjugated" materials are analyzed, including interviews with residents near Fernald, casual conversations with those on the periphery of power, certain nonnuclear magazine articles and news clippings, as well as the publications, press releases, and other revelations of the DOE and its recent Fernald contractors. Treating these sources as empirical evidence, linkages within the data are sought, as well as contradictions vis-a-vis official data and (in)formal interviews (e.g., former radiation workers and others affected by nuclear contamination). In this way, we attempt to achieve a more *balanced assessment* of the Fernald situation.

Deception and Secrecy at Fernald

The public problem of Fernald's nuclear radiation exposure is unsettling enough, but deception, if practiced in the past, adds an insidious element (Makhijani et al., 1995). For example, take the case of Daniel J. Arthur, who monitored safety practices at the Fernald plant from May 1984 until March 1986 (Brataas, 1986: A-20). Arthur stated that plant managers falsified data from water-well samples in order to conceal evidence of groundwater contamination. The well in question, No. 1 Shallow, was part of a protective pumping program, intended to intercept uranium contaminants that were migrating from a waste pit toward the plant's own supply wells. Arthur further noted that on November 27, 1984, No. 1 Shallow could not be tested because it had been removed from the ground; plant technicians told him that the pump had been out of the ground since June 1984. Yet "test data obtained by the *Cincinnati Enquirer* shows a recorded uranium value of 9 micrograms of uranium per liter of water for test well No. 1 Shallow on November 27, 1984" (Brataas, 1986: A-20). This November 27, 1984 value (which is within USEPA guidelines for uranium in drinking water) is reported in the 1984 Environmental Monitoring Report, produced by National Lead for the DOE.

Another relevant case is that of Herbert Kelly, who worked at Fernald for 27 years and then developed lung cancer (McKenna, February 4, 1990:A-1). On the one hand, Kelly relates, "I saw fumes out there so bad. Birds would fly out from roosts in the buildings and fly into the fumes and fall down dead . . . Hydrofluoric acid would overflow so often. Your shoes would get eaten off in a week" (McKenna, February 4, 1990: A-1). But Kelly was cautioned by plant officials never to talk about his work (i.e., that he should "button up"). Fernald's operations were classified throughout the 35-year tenure of National Lead, Kelly's former employer. He reportedly was told: "This is a military secret. If you're caught talking about it in a bar, or even to your family, you will be thrown in prison" (McKenna, February 4, 1990:A-1). In addition to these putative threats, he was apparently also told: "This won't hurt you," and "you'll live longer if you breathe this stuff" (McKenna, February 4, 1990: A-1).

The tragedy of this deception is driven home by the findings of two doctors, appointed eventually by the Ohio Industrial Commission, who stated that Kelly's lung cancer was directly traceable to his work at Fernald. Analysis of this evidence suggests that the perceived *need for secrecy*, coupled with power, led to deception and perhaps to the erosion of community trust.

Other contradictions emerge in the study of Fernald, which suggest that deception had negative psychosocial effects on the community. Louise Roselle, an attorney for plant workers and nearby residents in a class-action lawsuit, claims that plant officials never admitted any releases of radioactive cesium from Fernald until August 30, 1990, when the DOE reported that cesium-137 was detected in fish samples from a nearby creek (Higginbotham, August 30, 1990: C-2). A *Cincinnati Enquirer* article, on August 30, states that thorium-230, which has a radioactive half-life of 180,000 years, is also present in a waste silo and soil samples taken from the Fernald site. Yet Roselle points out that plant officials told the community previously that there was no thorium-230 at Fernald (Higginbotham, August 30, 1990: C-2).

No matter who turns out to be correct in these matters, it is curious that the DOE took from the fall of 1984 until August 1990 to admit publicly that cesium-137 and thorium-230 were present in and around the plant. Similarly, Lisa Crawford, leader of the Fernald Residents, finds it curious that she did not learn of her own well's contamination until 5 years after the first positive test by the DOE (McKenna, May 3, 1990: A-1). Regarding a more recent discovery of contamination in another private well south of Fernald, Crawford said, "They (DOE) knew in January, and here it is May? This is not right . . . They should notify people as soon as possible" (McKenna, May 3, 1990: A-1).

In keeping with Foucault's (1977) contention that in order to understand how power works, one should analyze the periphery of power structures where day-to-day decisions are made; an analysis of Fernald's local management is instructive. According to written testimony from a Fernald trial in Cincinnati (Kaufman et al., June 7, 1989: A-1 and A-6), the president of National Lead, which managed Fernald between 1981 and 1986, was not adequately aware of his environmental responsibilities. When asked in a deposition whether the US government is required to comply with environmental laws and regulations, NLO president, Fred W. Montanari, responded, "Not to my knowledge" (Kaufman et al., June 7, 1989). When asked whether he had received any federal DOE orders concerning environmental protection, he responded, "I'm not sure what a DOE order is" (Kaufman et al., June 7, 1989). Apparently, those operating on the periphery of the NLO power structure must have known more than Montanari. Montanari's testimony was important evidence presented by attorneys in a class-action suit on behalf of 14,000 persons who lived and worked within 5 miles of Fernald since operations began in October 1952.

A number of other plant-related issues are worth closer scrutiny. First, there are the discrepancies in DOE reports regarding the total amount of uranium emissions leaked into Greater Cincinnati's air during Fernald's 38 years of operation (McKenna, June 7, 1989: A-1). Estimates of uranium emissions into the air increased from 235,400 pounds (118 tons) in 1985 to 3,808,000 pounds (1,540 tons) by 1989. Second, energy expert Arjun Makhijani states (1991) that the latter estimate is low because Fernald personnel often did not check emissions at all. Third, calculations of the amount of uranium dust leaking from the plant may have been biased since they were based on overly optimistic scrubber efficiencies supplied by manufacturers of the pollution-control devices (McKenna, June 7, 1989: A-6). The calculation-ratio assumed that stack scrubbers removed 83 percent of the dust passing through them, thereby allowing 17 percent to vent into the air. With use, however, scrubbers lose efficiency such that increased emissions are released into the air. This uncertainty within leakage estimates has haunted DOE emissions reports since 1984 (McKenna, June 7, 1989: A-6). It also renders risk analysis much more difficult, if not impossible.

Regarding these problems, the US representative Thomas A. Luken (D-Cincinnati) found remarkable similarity between allegations the FBI investigated at Denver's Rocky Flats weapons plant and confessions of activity at Fernald that were filed in the class-action lawsuit against the Cincinnati plant (Associated Press and *Cincinnati Enquirer*, 1989: A-6). While Luken found it commendable that the Department of Justice (DOJ) and the DOE were investigating possible criminal activity at Rocky Flats, he also found it unfortunate that these agencies had not been as aggressive at Ohio's Fernald. Luken implied inconsistency—if not deception—on the part of the DOJ when he said that they were proud of their vigorous pursuit of the apparent cover-up at Rocky Flats but were simultaneously "turning loose a herd of lawyers in Cincinnati to deny similar activity that they previously bragged about" (Associated Press and *Cincinnati Enquirer*, 1989: A-6). Luken did not run for reelection in the fall of 1990 but was highly critical of the DOE for barring the press from accompanying him on a tour of Fernald in April of the same year (McKenna, April 12, 1990: F-1).

Other issues related to the plant itself should be mentioned and, in some cases, analyzed. Fernald officials now agree with critics that "some environmental factors . . . are affecting vegetation, fish, birds, and small mammals" near the plant (McKenna, May 25, 1989: A-1). In a study funded by Westinghouse, three researchers from Miami University of Ohio found abnormal growth patterns and genetic abnormalities in animals and plants living on the 1,050-acre plant site (McKenna, May 25, 1989: A-1), although a DOE contractor in Tennessee called the report "inadequate" and "fraught with statistical errors" (McKenna, May 25, 1989: A-1). Thus, there is no agreement, at this point, on what environmental stresses may be causing the problems. It is noteworthy, in this context, that the DOE wanted to buy beef from a local farmer, whose 130 dairy cows grazed on Fernald property, for the purpose of obtaining tissue samples for radiation research. The US Department of Agriculture performed tissue sampling on cattle within a 5-mile radius of Fernald in 1989, but the findings of that study were never published (Higginbotham, November 15, 1990: B-1).

According to Tom Carpenter (1989), then of the Government Accountability Project (Washington, DC), Fernald officials were interested in tissue samples from more than (lower) animals. In a letter to the editor of the *Cincinnati Enquirer* on May 22, 1989, Carpenter says,

> "It was Fernald officials . . . who literally dissected Fernald-employee corpses without the knowledge or permission of the families of the victims. In an agreement with coroners throughout Southern Ohio dating back to the 1960s, Fernald health-physicists were appointed "agents of the coroner" whenever a Fernald employee died, and therefore attended autopsies, obtained tissue-samples, and even the corpse of the deceased employee."

If *any* of the above is true, it would certainly suggest the existence of government secrecy and deliberate deception. However, as Foucault might have predicted, the "Fernald officials" mentioned in

65

the above accounts were employees of the site contractor—that is, peripheral, rather than part of the central authority, the DOE.

No supporting evidence of the above allegation was in hand when Carpenter's letter was published. A year later, however, upon learning of the death of Renae Cook, who had been a manager of Community Relations at Fernald, we learned that a "peripheral" official of our acquaintance seemed remarkably familiar with her medical history, including the unpublished fact that she had died of cervical cancer. Was this mere coincidence? Or does it suggest that Fernald officials may have known much more about the health problems of its employees than it admitted?

Subsequent to the publication of Tom Carpenter's letter, a 6-year-old letter was released by the *Cincinnati Enquirer* on June 11, 1991, that seemed to confirm 30 years of management cover-up of contamination risks at Fernald (Kaufman, June 11, 1991, p. D-1). It was written by Linda Munson, a consultant at Battelle/Pacific Northwest Laboratories in Richland, Washington, and addressed to Robert B. Weidner, then the director of NLO's Health, Safety, and Environmental division at Fernald. The subject of the letter was a proposed picnic for Fernald employees and their families at the Feed Materials Production Center. Munson referred to the picnic as "an extremely poor idea," since even the "clean zone" of the plant was contaminated. And if NLO were to take precautions to alert the visitors, Munson warned further, "Workers are very likely to learn that they have frequently been leaving the plant contaminated." She added that this would be a "more compelling reason" to drop the picnic idea than the likelihood of contaminating picnickers. Attorneys for the Fernald workers called the letter a "smoking gun," thus interpreting the letter as providing evidence that NLO kept employees ignorant of the risks of producing uranium for the Pentagon.

Possible Deception on the National Level

Assuming that at least some of the examples of nuclear deception noted above are valid, we turn now to the issue of the Fernald situation's generalizability. A thumbnail sketch of the US nuclear weapons industry suggests that Fernald and Rocky Flats comprise only the tip of the nuclear-deception iceberg (Cobb, 1989; Gallo, 1993; Schumacher, 1990). All seventeen of our nuclear weapons facilities have been secretive about their operations, but several situations deserve special mention because they tend to destroy community trust. For example, in the 1940s and 1950s, massive doses of radioactive iodine-131 were deliberately released across the Pacific Northwest from the Hanford Reservation in Washington State (Cobb, 1989: 433; Gallo, 1993: 11). These radiation releases came without warning, and some details are still classified. According to Magnuson (1988: 61), the reason for them was that Hanford's managers "wanted to see if they could reduce the amount of time uranium must be cooled before being processed into plutonium, presumably to increase production." As local farmer Tom Bailie put it, "We are victims of this mismanagement," and "I really think someone should go to jail for manslaughter" (Cobb, 1989: 433). In the view of Schumacher (1990), the fact that after several decades of denial, the DOE officially admitted the releases may serve to vindicate the claims of those who later developed thyroid cancer.

Similarly, two congressional committees have revealed that the Savannah River plant, in South Carolina, has experienced numerous reactor accidents that have been kept secret from the public for as long as 31 years (Gould and Goldman, 1990: 71-92; *New York Times*, November 2, 1988). Moreover, physicists termed the Savannah River accidents among the most severe ever documented at an American nuclear plant. In spite of claims that it was turning away from secrecy and deception, the DOE spent some 7 years during the late 1980s and early 1990s building a plutonium-processing center at the Savannah River weapons plant, without conducting public hearings or a formal review of possible environmental effects (*Cincinnati Enquirer*, November 10, 1990).

Continuing at the national level, several other nuclear problem areas deserve special comment: uranium miners in the Four Corners area of Arizona, Colorado, New Mexico, and Utah exposed to radon gas; communities in Southern Utah, Northern Arizona, and the American Midwest "dusted" by Nevada bomb tests, mostly in the early 1950s; and the tragic story of a nuclear incident that killed one scientist and injured several others.

From 1947 until the early 1960s, the AEC and the Public Health Service battled secretly over the safety of thousands of men who mined uranium for the US nuclear weapons industry. The result has been a legacy of disabilities and deaths from lung cancer across the Four Corners area of the American Southwest (Schneider, 1990: A-11). According to federal and state researchers, confirmed lung cancer deaths among the West's uranium miners could increase during the next 20 years. Dr. Victor E. Archer, principal investigator for the study of uranium miners from 1956 until 1979, explains, "Looking at it with the standards of today, you could take the attitude that the miners were being used as guinea pigs, and we were essentially watching them die" (Schneider, 1990: A-11). Initially, a serious health problem was the lack of radon-gas ventilation in mines. The AEC and mine operators rejected ventilation as "unnecessary and too expensive" (Schneider, 1990: A-11). Documents show that AEC medical officers discounted the danger of radon gas and kept influential researchers, such as Dr. William C. Hueper, from traveling to sites in the West after they spoke publicly about the problem (Schneider, 1990: A-11).

The case of the "downwinders" is equally tragic. Hundreds of people downwind from various nuclear weapons tests have been exposed to potentially damaging levels of radiation. Unfortunately for people living downwind from the Nevada Test Site (in Utah, Nevada, and Northern Arizona), radioactive fallout from bomb tests traveled far from the test site's borders (Fradkin, 1989; Physicians for Social Responsibility, 1989: 1; Robbins et al., 1991). Eventually, 8-10 percent of the underground tests had to be "vented" (i.e., radioactive gases were released from underground); therefore, NTS officials would not set off bomb tests when prevailing winds blew toward larger population sites, such as Las Vegas (Fradkin, 1989: 3; Physicians for Social Responsibility, 1989: 1). "Forgotten Guinea Pigs," a congressional report about fallout effect on downwind victims, concluded that the federal government chose to protect its atmospheric weapons-testing program rather than the health and welfare of area residents (Pendergrass and Nelson, 1987: 7). Many fallout victims have expressed the feeling that they were used as guinea pigs, and most were never told about the radiation hazards of nuclear weapons testing.

The case of Louis Slotkin and several other atomic scientists is both unusual and frightening (Honicker, 1989: 38-41 and ff). Slotkin received a lethal dose of radiation from the core of a plutonium bomb during an "incident" before the tests at Bikini atoll, in the Marshall Islands. One slip of a screwdriver on May 21, 1946, and 9 days later Slotkin was dead. One of the survivors, Allan Kline, was released from the hospital 2 weeks after the accident and was promptly fired (Honicker, 1989: 40). Eventually, Kline went to law school and tried for years to make the US government release his medical files from the incident. His efforts failed. All he learned was that his final diagnosis was "radiation sickness" resulting from significant radiation exposure at the time of the accident. Clifford T. Honicker, who wrote his master's thesis based on Kline, and several others were lied to repeatedly by the federal government. Senator Paul Simon said, "I don't know of any (other) cover-up that is this extensive . . . that could affect the lives of so many people" (Honicker, 1989: 103).

Legal Problems at Fernald and Rocky Flats

Not until uranium oxide was discovered in Lisa and Ken Crawford's water supply in 1984 did Fernald-area residents begin to understand some of the negative consequences of nuclear weapons production (Hardert, 1991: 7-10). In fall 1984, under the leadership of Kathy Meyer, more than 14,000 citizens living within a 5-mile radius of the plant formed FRESH. In 1985, Ken and Lisa Crawford sued the original plant operator, National Lead of Ohio (Murphy, 1990). The suit sought damages for the loss in value of Fernald residents' property and for the mental anguish they experienced. It did not seek damages for negative health effects, which had yet to be established by scientific study of the immediate area. More than 3 years after the lawsuit was filed, attorneys for National Lead acknowledged in court papers that there had been uranium leakages since the plant opened in 1951, that a total of more than 100 tons of uranium had been released into the Great Miami River, and that another 337 tons of uranium could not be accounted for. The DOE lawyers also stated that NLO should not be held liable for the radioactive leakage because NLO had operated the facility within the safety guidelines of its contract with the DOE (Hedges, 1989).

The US District Judge S. Arthur Spiegel requested a summary trial which began June 5, 1989. This courtroom procedure avoided the time and expense of a full trial (McKenna, June 4, 1989) and forced both sides to evaluate the relative strength of their arguments and the opponents' evidence. Attorneys for each side presented their best evidence to a six-person jury. The jurors' decision was not binding but indicated rather how a full trial might end, thereby encouraging the parties—at least putatively—to settle before the full trial started (Kaufman and Neus, June 8, 1989). Spiegel ruled that the chief executive officers of the companies named as defendants (i.e., NLO Inc., Fernald's former operator, and its parent company, NL Industries Inc.) must be at the trial. The defendants requested a closed trial, but Spiegel wrote in a court order that these "are matters in which the public has a vital interest" and decided to keep the trial open (McKenna, May 25, 1989). Plaintiffs asserted that their property values declined, and three homes were said to have lost $80,000, $40,000, and $10,000 in value, respectively. Fear of the Fernald installation reportedly left an estimated 50 percent of its neighbors with some kind of psychological disorder (Kaufman, June 13, 1989).

The summary trial jury awarded a $136 million verdict against NLO Inc. While not binding, it was strong evidence of public outrage over the vast environmental neglect in the nation's nuclear weapons program (Kaufman, June 22, 1989). The DOE, in assuming the defense for NLO, negotiated a $78-million settlement with Fernald residents to compensate them for the decrease in their property values, the costs of medical monitoring, and the emotional damage caused by their awareness of personal, long-term exposure to radioactive substances (Murphy, May/June 1990). A portion of that money was also made available to owners of commercial or industrial property within 5 miles of Fernald. The agreement stipulated that the DOE would deposit the settlement in Cincinnati banks by October 15, 1989 (Kaufman and Neus, July 1, 1989). The citizens' attorney, Stanley Chesley, also asked Judge Spiegel to require the class-action defendants to post a $156-million security bond. Chesley argued that otherwise "the United States and the defendant can treat a judgment enforcing the settlement as they have the settlement itself, by thumbing their noses at the court and ignoring their obligations to pay" (Kaufman, November 10, 1989).

When payment had not been made 4 months after the agreed-upon date, Judge Spiegel finally ordered the US government to pay $16 million of the $78 million within 30 days. He also imposed 10-percent annual interest on the unpaid portion of the settlement. On March 15, 1990, the DOE wired the promised $16 million initial payment. Attorney Chesley was quoted as saying, "The system works" (Kaufman, March 16, 1990). By December 25, 1990, seven thousand Fernald residents, who had spent 2 years working or living continually within 2 miles of the plant, were paid $500 each (Kaufman, December 25, 1990).

The legal problems surrounding Fernald were not over, however. Some six thousand Fernald workers filed a $1.6 billion lawsuit against their employer for alleged exposure to radioactive substances on the job (Murphy, May/June 1990). During June 1990, in a precedent-setting decision striking down the DOE's time-honored "sovereign immunity" (Manning, 1988), which protects the federal government and its contractors from lawsuits, a federal appellate court ruled that the state of Ohio could fine the DOE $250,000 for violating pollution laws (Russell, 1990). Subsequently, the Ohio State Attorney General Anthony J. Celebrezze Jr. filed contempt-of-court charges against the DOE and Westinghouse for allegedly violating a cleanup agreement (Murphy, May/June 1990). Finally, Energy Secretary James Watkins announced that Fernald would close down as a uranium foundry and that the EPA apparently would be the final arbiter in disputes concerning the eventual Fernald cleanup (Russell, 1990).

Rocky Flats facility also experienced legal problems. On March 26, 1992, the US Attorney Michael Norton announced that Rockwell International, contractor at Rocky Flats for the previous 14 years, had pled guilty to ten charges of violating federal hazardous waste disposal and clean water laws (Abas, September 30, 1992:15). Norton recommended an $18.5 million fine, which Rockwell executives agreed to pay. Rockwell's fine, however, was smaller than the government bonuses it won while operating the plant.

But the Rocky Flats legal story does not end here. The grand jury next wrote a report accusing the DOE of conspiring with Rockwell to commit and hide a number of environmental crimes (Lindsay, 1992: 7). The report brands the plant "an ongoing criminal enterprise," allowed to operate only with the complicity of government and corporate employees who "have breached the public's trust by engaging in a campaign of distraction, deception, and dishonesty" (Abas, September 30, 1992: 6). The grand jurors then submitted their report to the US District Judge Sherman Finesilver and expected the judge to make it public. To date, he has not released the document, despite a federal law that permits him to do so. In the meantime, Judge Finesilver has pressured the jurors to remain silent. To complicate matters, the grand jury also proposed indictments against both Rockwell and DOE employees, which the US Attorney Norton refused to sign, thereby rendering the indictments invalid (Abas, September 30, 1992:15). The result was a constitutional confrontation pitting twenty-two US citizens against Colorado's top federal prosecutor and his staff, the USDOJ, and Colorado's chief federal judge.

Early in October 1992, Colorado Representative Pat Schroeder wrote to Judge Finesilver, urging him to appoint a new grand jury to review the information collected during the Rocky Flats investigation (Abas, October 7, 1992:8). Ms. Schroeder also asked Finesilver to release the *original* grand jury's report, transcripts of testimony, and exhibits. Further, Representative Schroeder noted, "From what I can gather, the US Attorney did everything he could to sweep the entire scandal under a rug" (Abas, October 7, 1992:8). Members of a congressional subcommittee investigating Norton's handling of the case gave committee staffers the authority to issue additional subpoenas and decided to release complete transcripts of closed-door hearings they conducted in September 1992. Officials who appeared before the subcommittee have refused to answer most questions, however, arguing that justice department officials enjoy special protection against having to discuss their internal deliberations (Brinkley, 1992: 25).

And now, what are the implications for the environmental literature and for future policy debates regarding contaminated communities?

What Happens If We Continue To Go Nuclear

We have suggested that the previous literature on state regulation of environmental problems displays unacceptable myopia in its failure to recognize the potential of governmental actors, to be causes of serious environmental problems. Pollution resulting from nuclear weapons production at the US weapons complex has been discussed and debated publicly over the past few years, and DOE has now directed its attention to these issues. It has stated publicly that it recognizes their extent and seriousness and that it intends to expend vast resources to remediate past contamination and to establish sound waste management practices for the future (U.S. Congress, Office of Technology Assessment, 1991: 5). However, the Office of Technology Assessment (OTA) admits "that it may be impossible with current technology to remove contaminants from certain groundwater plumes and deeply buried soil, or even if possible, it may be extremely expensive or require prolonged periods of operation" (U.S. Congress, OTA, 1991: 6).

OTA's analysis shows that "whereas investing in promising new technologies may be productive, it should not delay immediate efforts to contain contamination that has the potential for wider dispersion or rapid migration and to establish programs that continually monitor contaminant movements" (OTA, 1991: 7). OTA also finds that "it may be more effective to invest substantial time and resources in the intensive development of a few technologies designed to address the most serious contamination problems than to make smaller investments in a range of potential innovations" (OTA, 1991: 6). OTA's analysis further indicates that "the DOE goal stated in the Five-Year Plan and elsewhere—to clear up all weapons sites within 30 years—is unfounded because it is not based on meaningful estimates of the work to be done or the level of cleanup to be accomplished at the end of that time" (OTA, 1991: 7). Further, without knowledge of the cleanup levels to be achieved by the end of 30 years or the technologies required to achieve such levels, DOE cannot develop reliable cost estimates for the total cleanup.

OTA (1991: 12) goes on to offer its own "Policy Initiatives to Improve Cleanup Prospects" at the weapons complex. These policies include

1. increasing congressional oversight of environmental restoration and waste management activities
2. enhancing the structure and process for assessing the public health impacts of weapons complex waste contamination
3. developing a structure and process to provide public participation in key cleanup policy and technical decisions (regarding the waste-pit cleanup at Fernald, e.g., see US Department of Energy, Oak Ridge Operations Office, 1990)
4. establishing a national mechanism to provide outside regulation of DOE radioactive waste management programs

But for some, this may be too little, too late, and there have been setbacks in the cleanup process. Cleanup delays at Fernald, for instance, cost the DOE $100,000 in fines, the largest ever paid to the EPA by another government agency (Willette, May 14, 1991). Further, a DOE memo indicates that there have been cuts in the budget for cleaning up waste at various DOE sites (Willette, April 19, 1991). Senator John Glenn interpreted these cuts to mean that "production is again being given a blank check at the expense of cleanup and at the expense of the Americans who face risks from exposure to dangerous substances" (Willette, April 19, 1991). Since the army found it too costly to clean up 1.4 million rounds of unexploded ammunition at Jefferson Proving Ground near Madison, Indiana (Cass, April 7, 1991), one wonders about the possibility of cleaning up the much more intractable military waste at Fernald. Testifying at a DOE hearing in Cincinnati, Arjun Makhijani (1991) said,

"It's time to stop using the word 'cleanup' because it's not honest. You cannot clean up Radioactivity—you can just move it around. Who wants it? Nobody wants it."

Perhaps this is why researchers David Pijawka and Alvin Mushkatel (1991) found so much resistance to the idea of locating a nuclear waste facility at Yucca Mountain in Nevada. Many Nevadans believe that the federal government is cowardly, incompetent, and disingenuous with respect to waste repository management and that the DOE used unfair and illegal procedures in selecting the Yucca Mountain site. The Pijawka and Mushkatel (1991) study examined several dimensions of public opposition to the proposed siting. This analysis suggests that the public's opposition to the siting, as well as their perceptions of the facility's inherent risks, result from a lack of trust in the DOE. Yet it is unclear whether those responsible for the siting program's failure to date have considered the issue of DOE legitimacy as a factor in the consistently high levels of public opposition.

The nuclear waste situation can be linked to the environmental policy literature in still other ways. Michael Edelstein (1988: 170-171), for example, refers to the "abject failure of prior state-of-the-art disposal practices," to the fact that 80-90 percent of our hazardous waste disposal sites are recognized as unsafe,; and to the reality that an array of environmental and human health hazards have been identified for every available waste disposal technology. This has led to a general disbelief in the ability of engineers to create and maintain safe waste facilities.

Thus, a second major implication of Fernald research is that nuclear technology, which engineers may not be able to operate without major incidents (Perrow, 1984), constitutes a "legitimation crisis" (Habermas, 1975) for the governments involved. In other words, technologies which must run without major incidents, which are essentially inevitable, can produce antiregime backlash when they begin to fail. Chernobyl East can quickly become Chernobyl West, and this possibility includes nuclear technologies in the United States, such as Fernald, and others sites located globally.

Similarly, Kurt Finsterbusch's description (Peck, 1989: 60) of the "reaction phase" within typical community response to hazardous waste exposure captures the entire Fernald experience of Ken and Lisa Crawford and others in the Cincinnati area.

> "The reaction phase found victims complaining and demanding actions from the authorities who usually acted slowly, stingily, and inadequately. The victims,

> therefore, had to organize and escalate their pressure on the authorities to investigate, stop further pollution, decontaminate, and compensate. Their pressure tactics were only partially successful. Meanwhile, polluters continued polluting an average 4.1 years after public discovery of the problem."

According to Finsterbusch (Peck, 1989: 60), the "resolution stage" of cases to date has tended to involve resolution of the immediate danger, with little removal of actual toxins. Waste pits have been covered, wells closed and/or capped, toxic emissions lowered to safe levels, and people have moved off contaminated land. However, few polluters have been prosecuted, fewer still have paid fines, and in the majority of cases, no victim compensation has been paid.

On July 16, 1991, interesting revelations were made by DOE and EPA officials at the Quarterly Meeting on Fernald, held in nearby Ross, Ohio.

This writer heard Leo Duffy, who heads the regional DOE waste management program, say that a million cubic meters of nuclear waste at Fernald remained for disposal.

This must be done because the plant is situated only 20-30 feet above the Great Miami River Aquifer, which supplies Southern Ohio with half of its water requirements. Duffy added that evaluation of the Yucca Mountain nuclear waste repository would take 20 years and that it would take 100-billion dollars to resolve the panoply of problems across the DOE complex. Members of the audience may have been relieved to hear Mr. Duffy state that the DOE had "made mistakes in the past" but that "we don't deal in deception anymore."

It is not surprising, nevertheless, that the local audience greeted this assurance with considerable skepticism. Community trust in Fernald, Westinghouse, and the DOE had been seriously eroded. It will not be restored, there or elsewhere, unless the promised cleanup is completed swiftly and effectively. The mood at the meeting was not optimistic, and news that improper equipment disposal by Westinghouse had cost Cincinnatians $400,000 and may cost millions more did not add to community optimism. Apparently, the most citizens can do to prevent governmental abuse of the environment and their health is to insist on public hearings and to reinforce the message by litigation when appropriate.

In conclusion, Michel Foucault's qualitative methods can be useful for studies of secrecy and deception in areas of subjugated knowledge, such as nuclear weapons production at Fernald, Ohio, and elsewhere in the nuclear fuel cycle. When political leaders in the United States encounter a poorly understood and potentially dangerous techno-social problem, it appears that they delegate it to a public agency simplistically, using a logic of bureaucratic organization. The latter necessarily entails neither the technological expertise nor humane motivation required for adequate resolution of the difficulty. This opens the door to ignorance, irresponsibility, secrecy, deception, and collusion among agency personnel, members of Congress, and on-site contractors. Meanwhile, the federal government penalizes state and municipal governments routinely for violating pollution laws.

On a more positive note, grassroots environmental organizations have had significant impact on communities affected by toxic disasters (Dunlap and Mertig, 1992: 3). Some research suggests that the psychosocial consequences of toxic disasters are as important as damage to physical health (Bachrach and Zautra, 1985; Edelstein, 1988; Glendinning, 1990; Levine, 1982). Akin to self-help groups, community organizations, such as FRESH, provide social support and mutual help, assist victims in understanding and channeling grief and anger, and offer a means for rendering the disaster experience meaningful (Dunlap and Mertig, 1992: 34). Some individuals—such as Lois Gibbs of Love Canal, Penny Newman at Stringfellow Acid Pits, Don Hancock at the Waste Isolation Pilot Project (WIPP) near Carlsbad, New Mexico, and Lisa Crawford near Fernald—become national leaders within the environmental movement. Further, the grassroots environmental movement is winning legislative victories throughout the United States, thereby expanding citizens' opportunities to participate in environmental decision-making.

Finally, the grassroots environmental movement influences how the US citizens think about the environment, government, big business, and public health. A higher proportion of Americans than ever before agree that environmental improvements must be made regardless of the cost (Dunlap and Mertig, 1992: 35). Citizen participation in these issues, as well as media coverage of local environmental struggles, plays an important role in increasing public support for authentic environmental protection.

References

Abas, Bryan. 1992. "Justice denied." *Westworld*, September 30-October 6, pp. 15-26.

Abas, Bryan. 1992. "Rocky Flats fallout." *Westworld*, October 7-13, pp. 8-10.

Associated Press and *Cincinnati Enquirer*. 1989. "Government probes nuclear arms plant." June 6, p. A-6.

Bachrach, K., and Alex Zautra. 1985. "Coping with a community stressor: The threat of a hazardous waste facility." *Journal of Health and Social Behavior* 26: 127-141.

Brataas, Anne. 1986. "Ex-safety official: Tests faked." *Cincinnati Enquirer*, October 19: A-20.

Brinkley, John. 1992. "Justice hinders house reviews of Flats probe." *Rocky Mountain News*, September 26, p. 25.

Caldicott, Helen. 1978. *Nuclear Madness*. Brookline, MA: Autumn Press.

Carpenter, Tom. 1989. "Fernald information must not be withheld." *Cincinnati Enquirer*, May 22.

Cass, C. 1991. "Dud ammunition being left behind." *Cincinnati Enquirer*, April 7.

Chambliss, William. 1978. *On the Take*. Bloomington: Indiana University Press.

Cincinnati Enquirer. 1990. "Plutonium plant tested in secrecy." November 10.

Clarke, Lee. 1989. *Acceptable Risk? Making Decisions in a Toxic Environment*. Berkeley: University of California Press.

Cobb, Charles E. Jr. 1989. "Living with radiation." *National Geographic*, June, pp. 403-437.

Colorado Council on Rocky Flats. 1993. *The Handbook on Rocky Flats*. Golden, CO 80401.

Crawford, Lisa. 2003. FRESH News. Vol. 33 (Summer): 1-8. FRESH Inc., P. O. Box 129, Ross, OH 45061-0129.

Douglas, Mary, and Aaron Wildovsky. 1982. *Risk and Culture*. Berkeley: University of California Press.

Dunlap, Riley E., and Angela G. Mertig. 1992. *American Environmentalism*. Philadelphia: Taylor & Francis.

Edelstein, Michael R. 1988. *Contaminated Communities: The Social and Psychological Impacts of Residential Toxic Exposure*. Boulder, CO: Westview.

Erikson, Kai. 1990. "Toxic reckoning: Business faces a new kind of fear." *Harvard Business Review* 90: 118-126.

Etzkowitz, Henry. 1984. "Corporate induced disaster: Three Mile Island and the delegitimation of nuclear power." *Humanity and Society* 8: 228-252.

Foucault, Michel. 1977. *Power/Knowledge: Selected Interviews and Other Writings, 1972-1977*. New York: Pantheon.

Fradkin, Philip L. 1989. *Fallout: An American Nuclear Tragedy*. Tucson: University of Arizona Press.

Gallo, Nick. 1993. "Nuclear nightmare." *Family Circle*, February 2, pp. 11-13.

Glendinning, Chellis. 1990. *When Technology Wounds*. New York: William Morrow.

Goffman, Erving. 1959. *The Presentation of Self in Everyday Life*. New York: Doubleday.

Gould, Jay M., and Benjamin A. Goldman. 1990. *Deadly Deceit*. New York: Four Walls Eight Windows.

Habermas, Jürgen. 1975. *Legitimation Crisis*. Boston: Beacon. Translated by Thomas McCarthy.

Hardert, Ronald A. 1991. "Nuclear exposure at Fernald, Ohio: You can't go home again." The Institute Report 3: 1 (Spring): 1, 2, pp. 7-10. Arizona Institute for Peace Education and Research. Tempe, Arizona.

Hardert, Ronald A., Mark Reader, Myron L. Scott, Gerald Moulton, and Alan Goodman. 1989. "A critical theory analysis of nuclear power: The implications of Palo Verde Generating Station." *Humanity and Society* 13: 2 (May): 165-186.

Hedges, S. 1989. "Bomb makers secrets." *U.S. News and World Report*, October 23, pp. 22-28.

Higginbotham, Mickey. 1990. "Reports reveal more hazards at Fernald." *Cincinnati Enquirer*, August 30, p. C-2.

Higginbotham, Mickey. 1990. "Officials seek to test Fernald cows." *Cincinnati Enquirer*, November 15, pp. B-1 and B-2.

Honicker, Clifford T. 1989. "The hidden files." *New York Times*, November 19, pp. 38-41 and ff.

Jakubauskas, C. 1991. "An inside view of the Rocky Flats plant." *High Country News*, March 25, p. 15.

Johnson, Carl. 1989. "Medical effects of nuclear weapons production." Presented at the Meeting of Physicians for Social Responsibility, Albuquerque, New Mexico, September 25.

Kaufman, Ben L. 1989. "Verdict in the summary trial reflects public's outrage." *Cincinnati Enquirer*, June 22.

Kaufman, Ben L. 1989. "Testimony challenged." *Cincinnati Enquirer*, Series: June 13; July 1; November 10.

Kaufman, Ben L. 1990. "DOE sends portion of debt for Fernald." *Cincinnati Enquirer*, March 16.

Kaufman, Ben L. 1990. "New round of Fernald payouts set." *Cincinnati Enquirer*, December 25.

Kaufman, Ben L. 1991. "Lawyers: Letter proves Fernald coverup." *Cincinnati Enquirer*, June 11, p.D-1.

Kaufman, Ben L., and E. Neus. 1989. "Gloomy report opens Fernald trial." *Cincinnati Enquirer*, June 8 and July 1.

Kaufman, Ben L., E. Neus, and M. A. J. McKenna. 1989. "Fernald's boss was in the dark." *Cincinnati Enquirer*, June 7, pp. A-1 and A-6.

LaGrone, Joe. 1989. "Statement of Joe LaGrone, manager of Oak Ridge Operations. U.S. Department of Energy, before the Subcommittee on Transportation and Hazardous Materials of the Committee on Energy and Commerce." July 5, pp. 1-29.

Levine, Adeline Gordon. 1982. *Love Canal: Science, Politics, and People*. Lexington, MA: D. C. Heath.

Lindsay, Sue. 1992. "Judge won't release Rocky Flats report." *Rocky Mountain News*, September 26, p. 7.

Magnuson, E. 1988. "They lied to us." *Time*, October 31, pp. 60-65.

Makhijani, Arjun. 1991. Testimony at DOE Public Hearing in Cincinnati, Ohio, on January 14.

Makhijani, Arjun, H. Hu, and K. Yih. 1995. *Nuclear Wastelands.* Cambridge, MA: MIT Press.

Manning, P. K. 1988. "Nuclear incidents: Accidents, violations of the status quo, or crimes?" Presented at the Society for the Study of Social Problems, Atlanta, Georgia, August 13.

McKenna, M. A. J. 1989. "Fernald trial to open." *Cincinnati Enquirer,* May 25, p. A-1.

McKenna, M. A. J. 1989. "Fear meets power in the courtroom." *Cincinnati Enquirer,* June 4, p. A-1.

McKenna, M. A. J. 1989. "Figures deceptive in gauging emissions." *Cincinnati Enquirer,* June 7, p. A-6.

McKenna, M. A. J. 1990. "2 Fights for ex-Fernald worker." *Cincinnati Enquirer,* February 4, A-1 and ff.

McKenna, M. A. J. 1990. "DOE shuts media out of Fernald tour." *Cincinnati Enquirer,* April 12, p. F-1.

McKenna., M. A. J. 1990. "Private well tainted by Fernald uranium." *Cincinnati Enquirer,* May 3, p. A-1 ff.

Murphy, Joan. 1990. "A non-toxic but still damaging leak." *Public Citizen,* May/June, p. 20.

New York Times. 1988. "S. Carolina A-plant hid 31 years of reactor accidents, probes reveal." November 2.

Peck, D. L. (Ed.). 1989. *Psychosocial Effects of Hazardous Toxic Waste Disposal on Communities.* Springfield, IL: Charles C. Thomas.

Perrow, Charles. 1984. *Normal Accidents: Living with High Risk Technologies.* New York: Basic Books.

Pendergrass, Gurli and Lorelle Nelson. 1987. *The Mushroom Cloud and the Downwinders.* Denmark: Forlaget Futurum and Physicians for Social Responsibility.

Physicians for Social Responsibility. 1989. "Troubled DOE facilities at a glance." 1000 16th Street, NW, Washington, DC 20036.

Pijawka, K. David, Alvin H. Mushkatel. 1991. "Public opposition to the siting of the high-level nuclear waste repository: The importance of trust." *Policy Studies Review* 10: 180-194.

Renshaw, Scott. 2004. "Swing Dance" and "Closing Time": Two Ethnographies in Popular Culture. Ph.D. Dissertation, Arizona State University, Tempe, AZ, August.

Rhodes, Richard. 1986. *The Making of the Atomic Bomb.* New York: Simon & Schuster.

Robbins, Anthony, Arjun Makhijani, and Katherine Yih. 1991. *Radioactive Heaven and Earth*. New York: Apex.

Ross, Jeffrey (Ed.) 2000. *Controlling State Crime*. New Brunswick, NJ: Transaction.

Russell, Dick. 1990. "In the shadow of the bomb." *The Amicus Journal*, Fall, pp. 19-31.

Schneider, Keith. 1990. "Uranium miners inherit dispute's sad legacy." *New York Times*, January 9, p. A-11.

Schumacher, E. 1990. "Radiation report is vindication." *Seattle Times*, July 24.

U.S. Congress, Office of Technology Assessment. 1991. *Complex Cleanup: The Environmental Legacy of Nuclear Weapons Production, OTA-0-484*. Washington, DC: U.S. Government Printing Office, February.

U.S. Department of Energy, Oak Ridge Operations Office. 1990. *Engineering Evaluation/Cost Analysis (Waste Pit) Responsiveness Summary: Feed Materials Production Center, Fernald, Ohio, FMPC .003.6*. Washington, DC: U.S. Government Printing Office, August. Prepared by Advanced Sciences, Inc., International Technology Corporation.

Wald, Matthew L. 1990. "Nuclear official gave false report, inquiry finds." *New York Times*, June 20, p. 12.

Willette, A. 1991. "DOE memo reveals cuts in cleanup budget." *Cincinnati Enquirer*, April 19.

Willette, A. 1991. "Fernald fine seen as victory." *Cincinnati Enquirer*, May 14.

CHAPTER 4

Psychosocial Effects of Secrecy at Fernald and Chernobyl

> I'm all for nuclear if we can make it economic and safe. Right now it's neither. It's catastrophically expensive. As for safety, if someone ever says to you that the nuclear industry is safe, just ask them this: If it's safe, how come they can't get insurance? It's not hippies in tie-dyed T-shirts who are saying nuclear isn't safe. It's the insurance industry, which is the final arbiter of risk in this country.
>
> —Robert F. Kennedy Jr.

Introduction

By compromising the integrity of individuals and society, radiation-related accidents challenge the authority structure upon whose maintenance the safe operation of the nuclear fuel cycle depends. Here, based on the personal interviews and English-language press accounts of the time, we examine some of the ways in which the 1986 Chernobyl nuclear accident set the stage for the collapse of the Soviet Union 3-5 years later. The chapter also employs interviews with individuals residing close to Fernald, Ohio, to examine the psychosocial effects of living near that plant after it ceased production in 1989. Readers may find similarities in the nuclear concerns of citizens living in different parts of the world.

Voices from Fernald

From 1951 to 1989, Fernald was a secret facility in Southwest Ohio, producing 70 percent of all uranium used in America's nuclear weapons (Creager, 2010: 1). The process was so secretive that Fernald workers did not know what their own colleagues did.

Yet in 2008, the plant reopened as the Fernald (nature) Preserve, complete with 7 miles of hiking trails and an attractive visitor's center. The trails are marked with radiation monitors, and dosimeter poles are evenly spaced across the property. The "Weapons to Wetlands" trail overlooks ponds and the mound, where 3 million cubic yards of radioactive waste is buried in a landfill covered with prairie grass. Fernald's most toxic debris was shipped to a nuclear waste dump in Texas. Visitors cannot see the ongoing cleanup of the Great Miami River Aquifer beneath Fernald. Pumps cleaning the aquifer will continue to do so until at least 2026 (Creager, 2010: 2), and the federal government will monitor air and water long beyond that.

Thus, Fernald is not a 1,050-acre preserve but also not a park. There will be no dog walking, picnics, camping, or picking up random rocks. As a tourist site, the Fernald Preserve is not at the top of vacationers' must-see lists. Little wonder that its neighbors make jokes about "fish with three eyes and birds with six wings."

Interviews: Being There

Most of our interviews took place between 1988 and 2005. Nancy was the first to mention the earlier Fernald signs and water towers with the red-and-white checkerboard design discussed in *Time* magazine (Magnuson, 1988). She did not recall exactly when the red-and-white insignia gave way to the blue-and-white ones, but Lisa Crawford, president of Fernald Residents, said that it was in 1986. When we asked Nancy how she felt about her government regarding the "incidents" at Fernald, she said,

> "I don't like it one bit. I think they should have been honest about what was going on out there. . . . In a case like this, we ought to know what is affecting our water, air, and the land around us. I just don't think it's fair."

When we asked Nancy if anything could be done about the Fernald situation, she replied,

"I think we ought to hold our public officials accountable regarding their positions before elections. If they promise one thing and do another, they should be held responsible for shifting their positions."

Later in her interview, Nancy related that some friends had a farm near Fernald, with cattle that had "died of mysterious illnesses." But "there was no foul play that could ever be proved." The cows just died off because "they were diseased." She also recalled "reading about a two-headed calf that had been born on a farm near Fernald."

Regarding a question about media coverage of events in and around Fernald, Nancy said,

"The media here (i.e., in Cincinnati) have been very informative. I'm sure that the pro-Fernald people probably aren't real happy with some of the media coverage, because they've been as honest as they can."

Next, we asked Marge how she felt about her government relative to its performance at Fernald. She replied, "Well, you *have* to trust them. I mean, who else is going to do it (i.e., build bombs) if they don't?" But Marge added, "If they've been lax, they should be taken to task for it." When we asked how this might be done, she answered, "Residents have to get off their fannies . . . off their duffs."

We asked Estelle how she felt about Fernald and her government. She seemed less trusting than either Nancy or Marge. We asked, "Are you happy with the situation at Fernald?"

She answered, "No, I'm not happy with *any* of it." Regarding potential solutions in the near future, she said that citizens have to get together and change things with "people pressure." We asked if that meant activist groups, such as Fernald Residents; Estelle responded, "Yes, people pressure. And if others sit at home and don't like it (i.e., community activism) and don't say anything, it's never going to change." What disturbed both Estelle and Marge, independently, was the revelation that three of the seventeen plants that build US nuclear bombs were located in Southern Ohio. The two women felt "surrounded with radiation" when they learned that the mound plant was located at Miamisburg, Ohio, and the Portsmouth Uranium

Enrichment Complex was at Piketon, Ohio, along with Fernald near Ross, Ohio.

We also interviewed Al who lived about 6 miles from Fernald. He appeared in relatively good health at the time, except for his bladder cancer. Al's neighbors, Florence and Lou, pointed out that their neighborhood seemed to have a high incidence of bladder cancer. Neither Florence nor her husband reported serious health problems, but their oldest daughter (now deceased) had breast cancer. Further, the woman who sold Florence and Lou her house also died of bladder cancer. Florence thought that many of her neighbors' health problems "were in the water," and the couple planned to begin drinking bottled water.

Al's interview was especially interesting because of his friendship with Joe, a truck driver in the Cincinnati area, who frequently made trips to Fernald. On one such trip, Joe's truck was "seized by plant security and kept at the plant." He was offered a change of clothing and a ride home. Fernald security offered no explanation for this behavior, but we were able to confirm Al's story by interviewing Joe. This validity check also revealed that Joe had been unaware of what was being produced at Fernald, other than his belief that the plant was "some type of foundry."

Probably, the most informative person we interviewed was Jack, who lived a little more than 6 miles from Fernald. He was a 33-year-old bricklayer with his wife and three children. His father had died of cancer several years before our interview, which might explain some of his interest in Fernald. Jack became our informant, confidant, and photographer. He knew many people in the area, and he was able to either confirm or deny information gathered from other local sources, including other interviews.

For instance, Jack knew about the two-headed calf mentioned in the interview with Nancy. He had friends who worked at a dairy farm near Fernald where the calf was born, and he got to see the calf shortly after it was born. We asked, "Was it stillborn"?

Jack answered, "Yes, and it was really weird-looking." He went on to explain that the land where these cattle were allowed to graze was part of Fernald's property. Jack said, "Yes, and it's *inside* the fence." He added, "Where it says 'No Trespassing,' there is also a sign that says 'Radiation' and signs that warn against falling." In Jack's photos, one can see some of the dairy cows wandering in and out of Paddy's Run creek, which turns through much of the Fernald property. Earlier, one of the dairy farmers had told Jack, "There is nothing alive in that creek, not even a spider." Thus, in the early spring of 1989, Jack and I walked along Paddy's Run, when the water was down, to see for ourselves. We spotted nothing alive in the immediate area of the creek—no water spiders, ants, tadpoles, or frogs. This might suggest that the creek had been used for toxic dumping either by Fernald or by other plants along the Miami River. However, when Jack asked one of his dairy friends if being so near Fernald had anything to do with the two-headed calf's defect, the friends said, "No."

Jack was also a great help in understanding the radiation monitors attached to the outer fences surrounding the plant. We wondered if the Board of Health or any other agency checked for radiation in the cows' milk, given the extra background radiation in the areas near Paddy's Run. Jack said that one of the local dairies was "borderline" on bacteria and artificial additives, but he was uncertain what radiation levels had to be reached before the "milk had to be dumped." This was an important question, Jack admitted, since some of the milk was being sold to the public.

*Black smoke at Fernald went unexplained
by plant managers after plant closed in 1989.*

Jack took photos of the cows and the radiation monitoring signs on March 19, 1989. The signs read "environmental radiation monitoring location," with a nuclear symbol on the lower right and the left sides of the sign. The radiation level reported on one of the signs was 0.007 millirems per hour. In other words, the DOE was admitting that this *added* amount of radiation was being released every hour to the normal background radiation that would have existed at the fences. When Jack and the author took photos of the monitors 1 week later on March 26, 1989, the reading had risen to 0.010 millirem per hour. Thus, the cows and the researchers were receiving additional radiation beyond average background exposure for that day in Southern Ohio in 1989. One can only speculate as to how much higher the radiation levels were for Fernald workers as one moved closer to the inside of the plant.

When we were taking photos at about noon on March 19, we noticed white smoke coming from the south side of the property. We then drove round to the west side of the plant and waited. Soon there appeared a large puff of dense, black smoke that Jack recorded on his 35-mm camera with a telephoto lens. This cloud of smoke dissipated rapidly, so we were "lucky" to have been there at that exact time. Jack had the negatives developed immediately, and one set went to Lisa Crawford, president of Fernald Residents. The second set went to a union official at the plant. Westinghouse, the initial cleanup firm at the plant, had no explanation for what might have caused the black smoke. The union official thought that the cloud of smoke might have been "steam" from the plant's whistle that was blown each day at noon. To test the union leader's hypothesis, Jack and the author returned to the west side of Fernald before noon on March 25 and waited. At 12:03 p.m. the plant whistle went off, but there was no attendant cloud of *either* black or white smoke.

Later, we took two photos near the south entrance to Fernald. One sign announced to visitors, "Official Business—No Trespassing." The front of a second sign read, "Warning, You Are Not Allowed Past This Point." However, the back of the second sign said, "Sensitive information is important, so Button Up." The latter sign depicts a mouth speaking into an ear in block art form, with the large words "Button Up" at the bottom. This sign cannot be seen by visitors entering the plant, but it can be seen by workers and others leaving the plant. During all the trips we made to the plant to take photos, even to walk in Paddy's Run, no security vehicles ever stopped us. We were on Fernald property at times, but not past any of the warning signs.

The next-to-last interview was with Roger, a designer who worked for a Cincinnati architect. He lived about a mile and a half from Fernald in a rented cabin. One of the curious features of his home was a toilet with a completely rusted bowl. All the porcelain had been eaten off by local well water.

During the interview, Roger mentioned that the Ohio Valley has a history of health problems and is considered to be a "cancer belt" due to its industrial location and its many chemical factories. An editor at the *Cincinnati Enquirer* verified Roger's claims about local health issues due to Fernald and various Ohio Valley chemical plants. The editor noted that Proctor & Gamble gave foreign workers disability pay *before* they moved to Cincinnati, perhaps to avoid future lawsuits over health problems. Thus, Roger wondered how we could do an adequate epidemiological study of Fernald, given the relatively high baseline cancer rate in the area. This was an excellent question, especially for a non-statistician. Several weeks after our interview with Roger, he sent us a photo of black smoke hovering over Fernald with the inscription: "More shit falls from the sky!"

Our final interview was with Gordon, who was a rich source of information regarding residents' psychosocial reactions to living near a nuclear weapons plant. This was partly because he lived within 5 miles of Fernald. As an older person, he had also had a lot of time to think about environmental problems and what might be done to alleviate them. When we asked Gordon about any emotional distress he had experienced due to Fernald, he said, "My whole life is one of trying to make this a better world, and Fernald didn't do the job." He explained,

> "If a person has emotional distress, then it seems to me like they would do something about it. And I did a lot. I spent a lot of time with peace organizations, some in the larger community. But there wasn't any within the 5-mile zone around Fernald."

We attempted to probe these ideas in the following exchange:

Q: So you're saying you cannot understand why others living near the plant did not do more about their stress?

A: Yes. They might want justice, but how much are they working to get it?

Q: I get the feeling you are a fighter. . . .
Have you had any problems related to Fernald?

A: Last week I was in shackles and chains. Is that a problem? Not for me it isn't.

Q: So you do a lot of demonstrating?

A: I planted a flower down at Fernald, and I got arrested for it.

Q: How did learning about the Fernald radiation leaks affect you?

A: One of the big effects was wanting to go to New Zealand, but I decided to stay and fight. . . . I joined with various antinuclear, antiwar, and pro-environmental groups.

Q: Is it true that a lot of Fernald neighbors were unaware that it was a nuclear weapons plant?

A: That's right. And sometimes I read now where the local farmers knew it was an A-bomb plant. Well, I lived pretty close and never had anybody tell me it was an A-bomb plant.

Q: It sounds as if there are very few people who have been as active as you have regarding Fernald.

A: Within the 5-mile area, I have only one friend who went down with me to sing and talk at small gatherings. But FRESH (the Fernald Residents) did a whole lot from a legal angle, and I supported that. They all lived in the area.

Q: You mean they acted as an organization?

A: Yes. They said, "Don't shut it down. Clean it up." And I said, "Shut it down and clean it up and keep the same people" (i.e., running it). FRESH seemed afraid that their neighbors would get angry if they said to shut it down. And the neighbors did get very angry at me when I said to shut it down. When I gave one guy a pamphlet through his car window, he threw it back in my face.

Q: So, the neighborhood changes affected you directly?

A: Well, people don't talk to me. But I get feedback that some of them don't think I was being patriotic. And they thought I was crazy for spending so much time protesting.

Q: Is your mind on Fernald pretty much every day?

A: When there's an action going on, it's pretty much 24 hours. In normal times, it enters my mind perhaps once every 2 or 3 days. Sometimes, if I'm eating my vegetables, I think about how much uranium is in them.

Gordon also noted that he didn't sleep much on nights before his court appearances, that his daughter always tried to "shut Fernald out of her mind," and that his unemployed engineer son avoided engineering firms "because most of them are doing war-related work."

Nuclear Nightmares

The Soviet people were sensitized to the dangers of the nuclear fuel cycle before the Chernobyl accident in 1986 (Weart, 1988: 366). What they did not know were the technical details of what transpires during a total reactor core meltdown. That, by itself, must have contributed to the high level of fear experienced in and around Kiev, and eventually all across Europe.

Well, before the partial core meltdown at TMI in 1979, nuclear scientists knew what conditions might lead to a major core meltdown. The essentials are described in simple terms for the layperson in *Mechanix Illustrated* (1979: 18-19). First, cooling water flows through the reactor pressure vessel before meltdown. Second, if a water pipe ruptures, control rods drop into the reactor core and the water level goes below the top of the reactor fuel. Third, the fuel overheats, forming a pool of molten uranium, and this starts to melt through the core. Fourth, the molten mass reaches the bottom of the pressure vessel, through which it steadily melts. And fifth, the melting continues through the floor of the containment building into the groundwater, or as in the case of Chernobyl, the meltdown blows the "roof" off the surrounding, factory-type building instead.

According to Spencer R. Weart (1988: 286-287), many Russian reactors were plagued by two technological weaknesses not found in American, French, German, and other reactors. First, some of the Soviet reactors, such as the damaged one at Chernobyl, were a graphite type in which "the chain reaction could run away" if the core temperature rose too high. Due to the laws of physics, a graphite reactor is especially suitable for producing plutonium for nuclear bombs. "Soviet civilian reactors were directly descended from the ones built to produce military plutonium, and they used many of the same design shortcuts" (Weart, 1988: 287). Second, Soviet reactors built before the 1980s—such as the one at Chernobyl—did not have protective, concrete containment shells. They had nothing more on top than a screen with holes, through which refueling took place. This made nuclear refueling easier and was economical.

Weart (1988: 287) characterizes the Soviet atomic program as "marred by sloppiness," . . . with a general disregard for the dangers of high technology, an attitude that had produced accidents in other countries. Authorities in the Former Soviet Union and its satellites "publicly insisted that there would never be a reactor calamity" (Weart, 1988: 286). To criticize a technology controlled by the state was equivalent to criticizing the state itself. The Soviet reactor program suffered more than one serious accident in which workers, and perhaps members of the public, were injured by radiation. However, "only vague hints of this came through the walls of secrecy" (Weart, 1988: 287).

Against this background, we now turn to discussion of interviews and news articles gathered immediately after the Chernobyl accident.

Voices from Chernobyl*

When Kirsten Waldthaler, 2 months pregnant, learned that radiation counts in the street water outside her home in Augsburg, West Germany, were abnormally high, she decided to visit her friends in Phoenix, Arizona, some 6,000 miles away. Several of Kirsten's middle-class acquaintances, whose situation was less urgent, simply gathered their children and went on extended holiday to Spain until the immediate danger of radioactive contamination had subsided.

Dr. Mark Reader contributed European interview data for this chapter after the Chernobyl accident.

93

"Were you afraid for your 5-year-old son?" I asked one of them. "Is that why you left?"

"My son, yes," she replied in a flash of anger. "But it was my health as well," she said, pointing to a skin rash above her right elbow. She had contracted the irritant after swimming in Lake Tegernsee at Bad Wiessee in the German Alps, where it had rained soon after the accident at Chernobyl. The rash had cleared up in Spain, she explained, but had reappeared on her return to Bavaria some months later.

How many others were physically and psychologically uprooted from their daily routines as winds and radiation-bearing clouds showered radioactivity across Northern and Central Europe immediately following the fire and explosion may never be known with certainty. According to the official reports at the time, the Soviets evacuated as many as 135,000 people from an 18-mile zone around the stricken reactor, forcibly moved twenty to three hundred Estonian reservists into Pripyat region to wash down contaminated houses and replace irradiated topsoil, and closed Kiev school 70-80 miles south so that thousands of children might go on early summer vacation far from the disaster scene. More certain is that for the first time since World War II, millions of Europeans, both East and West, lived in various stages of dread as they came face-to-face with a potentially devastating killer against which neither their senses nor their governments could apparently defend them.

In the days and weeks immediately following the Chernobyl event, telephone switchboards in both government and antinuclear offices throughout Western Europe were besieged by callers trying to find out if vegetables, milk, fish, and meat were safe to eat and whether their children might play outdoors without adverse health effects. In the streets and markets, consumers shared information about the risks involved in buying locally produced dairy products from suspected radioactive "hot spots." In Oslo, for example, a staff member of the Nobel Peace Institute told us that in the immediate aftermath of the disaster, shoppers and salesclerks had cooperated in identifying potentially contaminated cheeses by the factory numbers stamped on the cheese wheels. Brian Malloy of the World Information Service on Energy (WISE) in Amsterdam remarked, "We (meaning millions of Europeans) all became radiation experts overnight." Ten weeks after the accident, anxiety about the potential radioactive contamination of parts of the food chain remained high.

Walking through Helsinki's market, their stalls piled high with freshly picked bramble and blueberries, golden mushrooms, and brilliant flowers, we wondered if it were the terror of government-sponsored radiation poisoning that had cut American tourism in half in several European countries in July and August of 1986 and which had accounted for the 50 percent reduction in hotel room rates in Helsinki and Oslo. Tourism in Kiev was similarly affected, down for the year 1986 by 30 percent, with travelers there reporting the nonavailability of red and black currents, gooseberries, and mushrooms in late August and early September, a time when they are usually plentiful.

"It's so terrible because you can't see it, you can't smell it—it's just there," Olaf Johannson explained to the *New York Times* correspondent in Glen, Sweden, in September 1986 as he considered the impact on Saami (Lapp) culture of a government-ordered kill of fifty thousand reindeer contaminated after eating irradiated lichen. Rumors of birth defects among animals and of anomalies in flora and fauna were equally widespread. They were fueled by a lack of reliable information on radiation damage and unexpectedly high radiation readings in Welsh lamb, West German deer, and Norwegian goat cheeses, as well as by government warnings throughout Scandinavia against eating freshwater fish more than twice a week.

Could we confirm reports of birth deformities among rabbits and kittens near the Loviisa reactors, Pirko Lindberg, a Finnish journalist, wanted to know, anticipating by 3 years a report in the Soviet newspaper *Lenin's Banner* of the appearance of "giant green pines" in the woods near the damaged Pripyat reactor site or of reports of gigantism in leaves and flowers in other afflicted areas?

Similar stories had circulated in the United States after TMI and were again afloat as we departed for the continent in early July 1986. We told this to Lindberg, recalling Anna Mayo's *Village Voice* article. In it, Mayo had described being presented with several disconcertingly large maple leafs and a 30-inch pressed dandelion by residents living near the disabled TMI reactor. They would believe the strange vegetation had sprouted as a result of radiation fallout from the partial core meltdown at Harrisburg in 1979. Anxiety about the long-term economic and health effects of Chernobyl continued in Europe as the summer of 1986 waned, with motorists from Italy to Hungary joking openly to hitchhikers about the dangers of consuming homemade pastas and wines. Our Bavarian hosts worried openly about the purity of next season's beer crop and local meats, serving imported Argentine steaks instead of local beef.

We discovered, in our post-Chernobyl tour (of Finland, Sweden, Norway, Denmark, the Netherlands, Austria, and West Germany) in August/September 1986, that the only way of getting through daily life after the release of radiation into one's environment is to control one's imagination of disaster or to set it aside entirely. To do otherwise is to invite the very sort of paranoia and "psychic numbing" that Yale psychiatrist Robert Jay Lifton (Lifton and Mitchell, 1995) noticed decades earlier among the survivors of Hiroshima and Nagasaki. Three months after the Chernobyl accident, there was ample evidence that the European public was doing both.

On its surface, "out of sight, out of mind," seemed to be the most common way in which people had adapted psychologically to the long-term health and environmental hazards posed by the Chernobyl disaster. Literally, it was only in the mind's eye that we could "see" the absence of cattle in the summer fields of Central Europe during the first few weeks after the radiation release occurred or envisage the suffering of the dozens of persons who had already died, and would continue to die, of diseases spawned by the event.

As we boarded a liner in Stockholm for a summer sunset cruise across the Baltic, there were no signposts announcing that it was near here that alarms first sounded signaling the release of Chernobyl's deadly poisons. These poisons, according to official government claims, had probably contaminated many nearby farms and fields at great and long-lasting economic cost. As would happen to countless numbers of Americans after the 1989 *Exxon Valdez* oil spill in Alaska (Mayer, 1993), nature had suddenly become a disenchanted place.

In her *New York Times* review of East German writer Christa Wolf's post-Chernobyl novel, *Accident: A Day's News,* Eva Hoffman described the "interior mediation" of the autobiographically drawn heroine "as she goes through the ordinary motions of her day— working in her garden, visiting neighbors in her village, talking on the telephone to her friends and daughters" and "finds that in the light of Chernobyl, the most familiar details of her life have undergone a quiet, terrible mutation." The most "innocent elements of daily sustenance—milk, eggs, rain," a blue sky, a dandelion reflexively picked—all "turn eerily ominous." And yet within weeks of the accident, the markets of Europe were as crowded with people as they ever were, and children were playing as they always have, in the blowing but now potentially irradiated dirt and sand.

Indeed, ordinary Europeans seemed never to mention the tragedy in the Ukraine at all unless they were either asked about it directly or reminded of it by media accounts of other radiation-producing incidents. This had apparently happened in March 1987 following high levels of iodine-131 emanating from an unidentified source. "No people like to discuss their shame," a Kiev man explained to Alison Smale of the Associated Press in August 1986. But it is more than that. To admit to a 30-100-year invisible, everyday health hazard posed by Chernobyl would reopen an unresolved personal and political crisis of unmanageable proportions: incessant dread about the radiation contents of one's daily bread, the physical well-being of one's children, as well as the purity of the air everyone breathes. As Lifton (1986 May 18: E-25) noted in the aftermath of Chernobyl, in the presence of radiation-related incidents, many people become psychic survivors of the Atomic Age: Hibakusha, who in their imaginations, at any rate, are suddenly confronted with their own vulnerability and that of their species to a grotesque, invisible, and random killer.

"While one can speak of invisible contamination in connection with the exposure of toxic chemicals," Lifton (1986 May 18: E-25) observed a month after Chernobyl began, "radiation disasters have an added aura of dread associated with limitless danger, fearful mystery and images of Hiroshima and Nagasaki."

A fast-selling lapel pin being seen in an Olso market in the weeks immediately following the Chernobyl accident told the tale of near universal dread experienced in the wake of the accident. *Se Tsjernobyl og do.* "See Chernobyl and die," it read. Or as American entertainer Barbara Striesand explained to NBC Today Show interviewer Gloria Steinem, "It (Chernobyl) was like the beginning of the end of the world." Simultaneously terrifying and transforming.

"The literally inconceivable becoming reality," a traveler passing through Middletown, Pennsylvania, at the time of TMI, noted to a friend soon after the partial core meltdown there. Humanity face-to-face with the abyss, seemingly no better able to adjust to its encounter with nothingness than were the turn-of-the-century existential philosophers who had come before them.

The words of a 16-year-old girl who mistook a series of nonradioactive steam explosions at the Seabrook, New Hampshire, nuclear plant for an atomic bomb a few months after Chernobyl are indicative.

> "It was wicked scary. I thought it blew up and we were going to die. It sounded like a bomb, just like in the movies. We all jumped up. We thought we were going to get radiated. I called my mom and dad to say good-bye. I never felt that way in my life."

As writer Jonathan Schell (1982) had insightfully stated 4 years before the Chernobyl accident, that which makes life meaningful is a confidence that there will be others to both mourn and remember them after they have died. However, in situations of actual or imagined annihilation, as was present in the then mounting prospect of thermonuclear war, there is only the painful encounter with the void, a situation in which human purpose falls apart and individuals are reduced to a condition of childlike dependency upon any authority, religious or political, who promises them salvation.

It is not only the young who are victimized by nuclear terrors. Ever since TMI, we have *all* "lived in Pennsylvania," a metaphor for what has now become our collective encounter with the nuclear abyss. We can remember our despair when, in 1975, we learned that each of three planned Chernobyl-sized nuclear reactors subsequently built near our American Southwest desert homes would routinely contain a thousand times more radiation than was released at Hiroshima (Hardert and Reader, 1989).

Indeed, the more knowledgeable a person is about the routine health and environmental hazards posed by the errant atom (Bertell, 1985; Perrow, 1984), the more difficult the emotional adjustment to an actual or anticipated reactor breakdown seems to be. In part, this is because of an understanding that, with or without accidents, thousands of people will die prematurely over the next 30-40 years as a result of reactor malfunctions. Further, each reported radiation accident violates the personal and cultural autonomy needed for meaningful life.

"The whole story is that we thought Bangladesh was safe," Salahuddin Ahmed, a Bangladeshi, told the *New York Times* in explaining a "radiation panic" set off in his country more than a year after Chernobyl. This happened when local officials revealed that a 1,600-ton shipment of powdered milk from Poland was registering radiation levels higher than the officially sanctioned 300 Bq limit.

"With the Bay of Bengal to the south and the Himalayas to the north, we thought that if the Western powers got playful and started pushing buttons, rockets would fly right over us . . . (But) now we're getting hit by radioactive milk."

A similar picture of cultural violation, and unwanted dependency upon authorities, emerged among the Saami people as well. "The Swedish government pay(s) for the hay and buy(s) the contaminated reindeer meat," Pal Doj, a representative of the Saami culture, told a peace-related meeting in Japan a few years after the accident. "So we haven't suffered economically, but now we find ourselves totally dependent on the government's goodwill" (*Nuke Info Tokyo*, 1988: 4).

In these circumstances, even the most autonomous—and perhaps especially the most autonomous—of persons may experience emotional breakdown in the aftermath of a large-scale radiation-producing event. Thus, as a television interviewer led her to consider her recent pregnancy in light of the TMI accident, a seemingly self-possessed woman suddenly broke into tears. She decried having to rely on the very utility company executives, nuclear technicians, government officials, and media specialists whom she blamed for the accident and for information vital to her own health and that of her weeks-old fetus.

One would not expect that this woman's concern about the well-being of her apparently healthy baby, born some months later, to vanish after the immediate dangers of radioactive contamination had supposedly subsided. Thus, more than two generations after Hiroshima, health researchers found that among atomic bomb victims still developing illnesses from radiation exposure, "a cough, a change in weight, an unexplained fever can raise the fear of whether the time bomb set off in 1945" or in 1979 or 1986, for that matter, "has exploded" (*Arizona Republic*/UPI, 1989: p. A-11).

Apparently, once a radiation-producing incident occurs, many people are never fully free of the psychic wounds it inflicts nor of the social ostracism their victimization often entails, thereby complicating both their own and society's capacity to recuperate further from the event. This seems to be the case among survivors of Hiroshima and Nagasaki; teenagers worried about their sexual prowess in the aftermath of the Harrisburg disaster or those writing letters to the West from Hungary, Bulgaria, and Poland seeking information about the largely unreported health implications of the Chernobyl disaster, years after it occurred. It also includes citizens whose persistent fears about radiation poisoning (Sternglass, 1992) contributed to the 1989 decision by Soviet authorities to evacuate an additional 100,000 persons from villages in the Ukraine and Byelorussia up to 200 miles away from the damaged Pripyat reactor site.

If the public response to Chernobyl is any indication, the psychological helplessness which nuclear accidents engender seems to eventuate in various combinations of denial and rage. But personal denial was only part of the immediate post-Chernobyl nuclear syndrome as the emergence of a highly visible, grassroots, antigovernment environmental movement throughout Europe made clear. Indeed, from the time Chernobyl was first erroneously reported as having killed two thousand persons outright, the accident and its alleged mishandling by public officials have been as much a political as an ecological issue in both East and West (Sternglass, 1992: 10).

Popular suspicion of government-controlled radiation information was evident from the initial alert by Swedish authorities that something was amiss at Chernobyl.

"Chernobyl is everywhere—except in the East," a placard seen in a Krakow demonstration in June 1986 had read by way of challenging the general failure of former Communist Bloc governments to report on the accident at all.

A May 6, 1986 letter issued by the Moscow Trust Group and addressed to "all friends and colleagues in independent peace movements of West and East" captured the anger of many citizens over governmental mishandling of radiation health information in the days immediately following the disaster:

> "The catastrophe at the Chernobyl power plant has awoken us to the inherent dangers of the so-called peaceful applications of nuclear energy . . . We, the Trustbuilders, have obtained bits of news about the catastrophe which are hard to find . . . We insist that all Soviet nuclear power stations be stopped . . ."

Demands for details about radiation fallout were also recorded in local communities in Poland, Czechoslovakia, East Germany, and Yugoslavia at about the same time and are generally credited with slowing subsequent nuclear energy development plans in these nations. In May 1986, for example, factory workers in Warsaw complained bitterly about the Polish government's failure to inform them about the "danger of radiation and preventive measures until 4 days after the disaster . . ."

"Our children could have been given iodine a day or two earlier—when they needed it most," the angered workers charged (Across Frontiers, Fall, 1986).

Similarly, one of several widely circulated grassroots documents thought to have precipitated an "unprecedented debate" within Protestant churches and grassroots organizations about energy futures in the then German Democratic Republic (GDR) pointedly indicted governing scientific and political elites in the United States, the Former Soviet Union, and their own country for monopolizing vital radiation information to "tranquilize public opinion with banal assertions of confidence in nuclear energy and plant safety and by whitewashing the reactor catastrophe."

In Czechoslovakia and Yugoslavia, public protests took a slightly different turn. Charter 77 human rights activists attacked the failure by officials to provide "any medical or hygienic instructions or measures" in the critical days following the calamity, while Yugoslavian counterparts chastised their government for not warning their citizens about the local fallout during May Day celebrations when much of the nation had gathered outdoors to honor the workers' state. The subterfuge, Yugoslavian protesters alleged, was carried out in order to protect their country's tourist industry, agricultural exports, and four planned (and since cancelled) nuclear reactors.

Popular suspicion of governments' manipulation of radiation data in order to maintain their authority was not confined to these formerly Communist Bloc nations. An American living in Rome when Chernobyl first happened voiced what seems to have been a common, cross-national disbelief of *all* government-authored radiation fallout information. Writing in the *Atlantic* (1987), Mary Jo Slater accused governing elites throughout Europe of cloaking the entire continent in a "cloud of secrecy" and misrepresentation about what she and others believed were dangerously high levels of radiation in the food chain.

Slater's (1987) charges were given substance a few months later with the discovery in West Germany of 150 railroad carloads of irradiated dried milk destined to be turned into animal feed for export to Egypt, Angola, and possibly other Third World countries. And despite radiation concentrations reportedly more than sixteen times the European community's maximum permitted dose for humans, and more than four times the maximum for animal feed, Bavarian officials initially had refused the return of the irradiated milk, arguing that it could be mixed with other animal feed and safely sold for livestock consumption on the world market (*New York Times*, January 31, 1987).

The irradiated dried milk controversy was back in the international headlines at Easter time, 1987, following the discovery and confiscation of packaged irradiated chocolate bunnies and rabbits from 189 West German nursery schools (*Arizona Republic*, April 9, 1987). Nor was Slater (1987) alone in her suspicions that several Western governments had routinely concealed the presence of radiation in the global food chain as a result of the Ukrainian disaster.

In the weeks and months following the tragedy, grassroots radiation information networks began to distribute lists of radiation-tainted foodstuffs throughout many parts of Europe. Argentina, Singapore, Malaysia, and Brazil rejected shipments of irradiated Polish potatoes, milk products from the Netherlands and Denmark, wheat from Italy, and imported milk from West Germany, Denmark, and the Netherlands, respectively, on the grounds that their radiation content was too high (Tagliabue, 1987). And amid signs that a spontaneous, worldwide boycott of European produce had begun, the US-based company, H.J. Heinz, attributed a large jump in its net income for the fourth quarter ending April 1986 and for the whole of 1987 to the fact that Chernobyl had "caused people to stop eating fresh food."

Nuclear Skepticism

The degree of public mistrust of official estimates of radiation damage caused by Chernobyl seems to have been a function of several factors: economic interest, class, sex, age, nationality, confidence in elected officials, attitudes toward authority in general, belief in the reliability of media, and the availability of radiation information itself.

As several Finnish peace activists informed us, those who tended to minimize long-term radiation hazards in their country, as most did, were men, often soldiers, and women "who like to be taken care of."

In the Netherlands and Denmark, the story was somewhat different. Citizens there initially seemed quite willing to believe they were spared serious radiation damage as a result of Chernobyl, even though the government of Thailand banned the sale of dried milk imported from these countries in November 1986 because of their excessive radioactive content. What concerned the Dutch and Danish population more than dried milk was the ability of the French to manage their nuclear technologies. This included the 5,200-megawatt Cattenom facility across the border from Luxembourg. Also of concern were the West Germans, with twenty reactors, a partially constructed waste plant at Wackersdorf, and the Kalkar regeneration facility in North Rhine-Westphalia.

On the other hand, as was the case after TMI, Europeans who seem to have adapted least well in Chernobyl's aftermath were highly educated laypersons, many of whom were aware that even under the best circumstances uranium-produced electricity cannot be produced without some negative impact on human life and the environment.

"I was not much interested in the nuclear power question until the Soviet accident happened," a West German anesthesiologist in his mid-thirties apologized. "But now it is consuming every moment of my time. I am more and more concerned about what I eat and drink. . . . We simply do not have enough independent researchers and equipment to measure the fallout in any reliable way."

Members of the Moscow Trust Group expressed a similar feeling of impotence in the face of a radiation killer against whom neither their senses nor their government were willing or able to defend them. "We insist on the use of the mass availability of low-priced, individual radiometers for Soviet citizens and visiting tourists," they asserted, "so that real risks can be avoided and undue panic is impossible."

In the West, anger about the reliability of government-produced radiation information appeared to run deepest among the ecologically minded (Die Gruenen) in West Germany, who staged several mass demonstrations against continuing the nuclear option immediately after the accident. The young, the professional classes, and dissenting members of the scientific and intellectual communities had reason to believe that either they or others were being injured by government and nuclear industry disinformation.

"Find out if people trust their governments," Dr. Carl Johnson advised. A respected radiation researcher and prominent nuclear whistle-blower before his death in 1989, Dr. Johnson had been fired from his job as Jefferson County, Colorado, health director after linking elevated cancer rates in the Denver area in the 1970s to several plutonium fires at the nearby Rocky Flats nuclear weapons plant a generation earlier (Johnson, 1981).

"I was always against nuclear power without knowing why," Marjo Liukkonen, twenty-seven, a journalism student at Tampere University in Finland confided. "Many of us were at an antinuclear rally when we heard about the accident. And then I knew why. But the government told us not to be afraid, not to worry about the radiation." "I went home (to my 2-year-old daughter) and thought about what I could do," she continued. "I read that Finland's population was declining." And so I decided "if they (the authorities) do not care about children, then why should we give birth to them?"

Marjo started the Finnish birth protest movement soon after, persuading four thousand Finns, including many men, to sign a petition not to procreate until nuclear reactors were removed from Finland. "I knew that some (who signed the petition illegibly) were afraid of their job futures," Marjo concluded, "but they signed anyway."

We detected similar doubts about the reliability of radiation data supplied by nation/state politicians during a visit to the IAEA in Vienna. A few weeks before Soviet scientists released their initial Chernobyl radiation findings to the international community, IAEA officials informed us that they were totally dependent on member states for radiation-related information, and as far as IAEA scientists could ascertain, initial radiation readings from Chernobyl were taken at the sites of immobile, preexisting facilities rather than where radiation fallout may have actually occurred.

Given the uncertainties about the actual and eventual Chernobyl casualties, a West German movie director who joined the "greens" immediately following the catastrophe stated that when it comes to radiation-related statistics, "nobody really trusts anybody," and because they do not, most people would prefer to just forget about the accident.

Death in Slow Motion

But forgetting was, and is, not always easily done. Continuing public anxiety about the long-term legacy of Chernobyl was fueled by several factors: suspicion that more than the officially designated thirty-one persons died as a direct result of the disaster, wildly fluctuating estimates of eventual accident casualties, and mounting evidence that modern governments—both East and West—continued to routinely lie about the seriousness of subsequent nuclear mishaps. Most important was the Gorbachev government's insistence that the accident demonstrated how much worse a nuclear war would be.

Indeed, popular resentment about the downplaying of the accident's health costs seems to have reached such proportions in the Soviet Union that, on the third anniversary of the disaster, officials there found it necessary to label a "phobic" those with widespread fears about the potential radioactive contamination. Soviet officials also imposed strict controls on the broadcasting and publication of information about nuclear and other energy-related accidents. However, popular fear of radioactive contamination in the Former Soviet Union had apparently reached such intensity by 1989 that under public pressure from its readers, *Pravda* finally published maps of the areas of Byelorussia, Ukraine, and the Russian republic hardest hit by radiation.

"We can no longer avoid the fact that there is a possible connection between (Chernobyl) and an increased number of (recorded birth) deformities" in West Germany. Karl Sperling of the Human Genetics Institute of the Free University of Berlin had concluded a year after Chernobyl, articulating a commonly held view. Contributing to people's misgivings about the trustworthiness of official injury estimates was disputes about the seriousness of the accident within scientific circles in general. Scientific estimates of eventual Chernobyl casualties worldwide were most notable, ranging from lows of zero to one thousand persons to one million excess cancer deaths and illness over a 30-year period.

As contentious as some of Dr. John Gofman's claims (US Committee of Nuclear Responsibility) were, their impact on government credibility may have been given added weight in 1990 when, after a 10-year battle, the US Establishment scientists finally admitted that, after TMI, their predecessors had set the permissible low-level radiation threshold for nuclear workers and the public at large at too low a level by three to fifty-six times.

While disagreeing with Gofman's extrapolations on several grounds, other scientists were also expressing concern about the negative health legacy of radioiodines on the global population. In an article written for the usually pro-nuclear *EPRI Journal*, for example, Richard Vogel, senior advisor to the Electric Power Research Institute, noted that Soviet scientists had "estimated that over 7 million curies of the short-lived radioiodine were released at Chernobyl, in comparison with the 10-20 curies at TMI." Further, in a study of Marshall Islanders issued a short time later, Dr. Thomas Hamilton suggested that those who had survived the 1954 Bikini Atoll hydrogen bomb tests were experiencing thyroid abnormalities from radioactive iodine at a rate thirty-three times higher than that had been estimated by US government scientists.

Coloring the public's perception of the long-term medical consequences of Chernobyl are several additional radiation-health studies concerning leaky nuclear plants released in the accident's aftermath. In the United States, for instance, researchers found cancer clusters seven times higher than expected in rural areas around the TMI facility. And a 1987 report by Jim Ruttenber, an epidemiologist for the federal Center for Disease Control in Atlanta, claimed that between 1944 and 1953, twenty thousand children living near a government-operated plutonium plant at Hanford, Washington, were exposed to the highest doses of radiation since the nuclear age had begun.

Speaking to the common sense of the matter at the time of the Chernobyl accident, Dr. Alice Stewart, another epidemiologist with the Department of Social Medicine at Birmingham University, UK, who was lecturing at Portland State University, expressed alarm that Portland's water had reached its highest levels of radioactivity since the early 1970s.

By way of contrast, Dr. Robert Gale, the American doctor who performed bone marrow surgery on several Russian Chernobyl accident victims, reported in November 1986 that the more conventional Soviet long-term death projection of between 5,000 and 75,000 could be too high "by a factor of 10," although genetic damage caused by the event might be more substantial than previously supposed and elevated radiation readings might last in parts of Europe for as long as 300 years.

Continued suspicion about government's handling of radiation information has been fueled by a series of charges that French, Japanese, West German, US, and Soviet authorities concealed additional radiation leaks from the public since Chernobyl (as recent examples, see *Arizona Republic*, August 10, 2004; Geranios, 2004; Shaffer, 2004). For instance, a radiation leak at a nuclear reactor in Hamm, West Germany, days after Chernobyl was hidden from the public until the end of May 1986 "while increases in local radiation were attributed to the fallout from Chernobyl" (Walker, 1986). This was followed soon after by serious allegations from nuclear critic, Dr. Rosalie Bertell, president of the board of directors of the International Institute of Concern for Public Health, that the United States had used the radiation fallout from Chernobyl to conceal its own radiation venting from an unsuccessful Star Wars test (believed to have been "Mighty Oak" on April 10, 1986) in the Nevada desert. Bertell also charged that West Germany, France, and Japan had also used Chernobyl to cover up excessive venting from their nuclear reactor programs at about the same time.

Two years later, in December 1986, the West German government was again being accused of irresponsibility in its reporting of radiation leaks, this time by political parties critical of an official, previously unannounced decision to downgrade the seriousness of a several-month-old Frankfurt atomic power plant accident that had released radioactive steam into the atmosphere.

Indeed, since the Chernobyl disaster, revelations of the superpowers' deceit in failing to report radiation accidents throughout the nuclear age have become commonplace, largely as a result of the cumulative impact of independent researchers and press accounts in the West and in Mikhail Gorbachev's perestroika policies in Eastern Europe. For example, it was not until 1988-1990, almost five decades into the Atomic Age, that the Soviets finally confirmed that a massive radiation explosion had occurred at a waste dump in the Urals in 1957 and that US officials admitted that the cleanup cost of its supposedly unpolluted atomic weapons program alone might cost $200 billion over a 60-year period.

Despite their apparent candor in revealing past shortcomings in the operation of their nuclear arms and electric power programs, nuclear regimes have continued to conceal the full dimensions of their nuclear rule from public view. Thus, even as it acknowledged the need for government-led health studies as a result of past breakdowns in its nuclear arms program, the US officials have regularly fought a rear guard action to prevent independent researchers from gaining access to the medical records of nuclear workers and those members of the public allegedly exposed to radiation mishaps over a 45-year period.

Nor did Moscow fare any better under Soviet rule. This in December 1990 in what was to prove the first of many such accusations of nuclear failures, the German news magazine, *Der Spiegel,* quoted a former engineer at the Lubmin, East German plant, as claiming that a Chernobyl-sized disaster at a Soviet-built reactor had been narrowly averted in 1976 when a fire had disabled five of six of the facility's backup cooling pumps.

Given these and related incidents, it is not surprising that many people believe that the Chernobyl tragedy has already killed more than its thirty-one initial deaths and led to the apparent suicide of Soviet Academician Valery Legasov, who was also among those involved in efforts to seal the failed reactor, 2 years later. In an interview given to the *Moscow News* shortly before his death, Legasov condemned those Soviet officials who believed "that there is no science without victims" and called for an end to "secrecy on things for the making of correct decisions."

Ukrainian nuclear physicist Vladimir Tschernosenko, in a recent book, refers to Chernobyl as being one of the major forces in the collapse of the Communist system. Meanwhile, the IAEA, based in Vienna, Austria, continues to downplay the impact of the 1986 event. Tschernosenko says politicians decided to put the remaining three reactors back on line regardless of the cost, and he describes the reality gap between what the Soviet press reported and the actual happenings. Between 650,000 and 1 million "liquidators" (the Soviet term) worked in the "hot zone" over the 5 years following the catastrophe. Five to seven thousand of them are already dead and at least fifty thousand more are invalids. The Austrian news magazine *Profil*, in examining this book, continues to mention the 135,000 people evacuated from a 30-km zone, who are not being medically controlled after exposure to the highest levels of radiation. We shall no doubt learn much more from Chernobyl in the future. Will we take the lesson seriously?

References

Across Frontiers. 1986. "Factory workers in Warsaw complain about radiation dangers." Fall.

Arizona Republic. 1987. "West German official recalls tainted chocolate." April 9.

Arizona Republic (UPI). 1989. "Atomic bomb victims." June 17, p. A-11.

Arizona Republic (Associated Press). 2004. "Four die in Japan nuclear plant accident." August 10, p. A5.

Bertell, Rosalie. 1985. *No Immediate Danger*. Ontario: Women's Press.

Creager, Ellen. 2010. "Once notorious uranium waste site in Fernald, Ohio, beckons tourists." June 13, Freep.com.

Geranios, Nicholas K. 2004. "Nuclear workers win support." *Arizona Republic*, July 17, p. A-12.

Johnson, Carl. 1981. "Medical Effects of Nuclear Weapons Production." Presented at the Meeting of Physicians for Social Responsibility. Albuquerque, New Mexico, September 25.

Hardert, Ronald A., and Mark Reader. 1989. "A critical theory analysis of nuclear power: The implications of Palo Verde nuclear generating station." *Humanity and Society*, Vol. 13, No. 2, pp. 165-186.

Lifton, Robert J. 1986. "Chernobyl, Three Mile Island, Hiroshima," *New York Times*, May 18, p. E-25.

Lifton, Robert J., and Greg Mitchell. 1995. *Hiroshima in America: Fifty Years of Denial*. New York: G. P. Putnam.

Magnuson, E. 1988. "They lied to us." *Time*, October 31, pp. 60-65.

Mayer, Michelle. 1993. "All the Kings Horses": Community Response to the Exxon Valdez Oil Spill. Honors thesis at Arizona State University, Tempe, AZ, November 30.

Mechanix Illustrated. 1979. "What really happens in a meltdown." August, pp. 17-19 and 98-100.

New York Times. 1987. "Bavarian officials refuse return of irradiated milk." January 31.

Nuke Info Tokyo. 1988. "Peace meeting." June, No. 5, p. 4.

Perrow, Charles. 1984. *Normal Accidents: Living with High Risk Technologies*. New York: Basic Books.

Schell, Jonathan. 1982. *The Fate of the Earth*. New York: Alfred Knopf.

Shaffer, Mark. 2004. "Governor wants inquiry after nuclear packing material leak." August 21: B9.

Slater, Mary Jo. 1987. "Italy: living with fallout." *Atlantic*, January, pp. 30-35.

Sternglass, Ernest. 1992. "Early infant deaths from nuclear fallout." *Atoms and Waste*, Vol. 2, No. 4, pp. 1-10.

Tagliabue, John. 1987. "A nuclear taint in milk set off German dispute." *New York Times*, January 31, pp. 1 and 4.

Walker, Martin. 1986. *The Waking Giant: The Soviet Union under Gorbachev*. London: Michael Joseph.

Weart, Spencer R. 1988. *Nuclear Fear: A History of Images*. Cambridge, MA: Harvard University Press.

CHAPTER 5

Regulatory Failure at Fernald, Chernobyl, and Fukushima

I'm not a writer. I won't be able to describe it. My mind is not enough to understand it. And neither is my university degree. There you are: a normal person. A little person. You're just like everyone else; you go to work, you return from work. You get an average salary. Once a year you go on vacation. You're a normal person! And then one day you're turned into a Chernobyl person. Into an animal, something that everyone's interested in, and that no one knows anything about. You want to be like everyone else, and now you can't. People look at you differently. They ask you: was it scary? How did the station burn? What did you see? And, you know, can you have children? Did your wife leave you? At first we were all turned into animals. The very word Chernobyl is like a signal. Everyone turns their head to look at you. He's from there!

—Svetlana Alexievich (*Voices from Chernobyl*)

Introduction

The author of this book was involved in a case study of a Southwestern US nuclear power station (Hardert, 1989) two decades ago. They found that several types of conflict theory explained what they saw transpiring at the Palo Verde Nuclear Generating Station near Wintersburg, Arizona. These findings influenced their theoretical interpretations of what went wrong both at Fernald and at Chernobyl.

The more these authors observed the development of Palo Verde, the more they were attracted to the critical theory of Jürgen Habermas (1975) and the structural sociology of Michel Foucault (1977) as an explanation of nuclear power development in Arizona. Analyzing Palo Verde within a framework of critical theory and structural sociology concepts (such as domination, control, technical repression, distortion, and contradiction) gave them a more compact and meaningful way of understanding the workings of the US nuclear electric industry within the context of social power (Hardert, 1989). These concepts, taken together, provide a critique of the political and social domination that operates within the entire nuclear fuel cycle.

This chapter is part of a larger inquiry into how decisions involving the production and use of so-called "high" technologies in modern societies can contribute to legitimation (authority) problems for the political and economic elites that promote them. Using publicly available information provided by scholars and the media—along with in-depth interviews of grassroots nuclear activists from around the United States, Canada, and post-Chernobyl Europe—this analysis suggests that the degree of antigovernment sentiment among local environmentalists around the world has as much to do with their general definition of social justice as with their own victimization due to the technological choices of the authorities. It is within this framework, the authors conclude, that social researchers may discover the extent of their own and of others disaffection with the dominant social paradigm. In this context, they may begin to understand some of the pressures that impel technological elites to discredit and, if need be, criminalize those who oppose them.

Technological Civilization and the Legitimation Crisis

This chapter was given impetus by several closely spaced social events, each of which raised some troubling questions about the complex relationship among crime, punishment, and the professional responsibilities of social scientists in an emerging, global-technological civilization.

The first of these circumstances was the appearance in 1993 of a number of new reports revealing, belatedly, government deceptions that jeopardized the health and safety of unsuspecting citizens at the dawn of the Atomic Age (Welsome, 1999). The most striking of these accounts told of at least five previously undisclosed experiments, conducted around the United States in the early 1950s, in which approximately 235 infants were injected with radioactive iodine to study the thyroid function in newborns (Scripps, 1993). Added to this was the reported discovery of a previously suppressed memo, written in 1950 by a US government scientist, that likened (then) proposed radiation testing on humans to experimentation in Nazi concentration camps (*Boston Globe*, 1993).[2] Three other articles, all published about the same time, described American and former Soviet government suppression of information about additional radiation experiments. These consist of a dozen secret tests conducted in New Mexico, Tennessee, and Utah from 1948 to 1952, in which radiation was released in various ways on unsuspecting US citizens (Rizzo, 1993); concealment of more than two hundred nuclear weapons tests and about eight hundred radiation tests on humans, including eighteen civilians who were injected with plutonium in the 1940s, to see what radiation doses workers might be exposed to safely (Herbert, 1993; *New York Times*, December 18, 1993); and the revelation (*New York Times*, November 7, 1993) of how 45,000 Soviet military personnel were deliberately exposed to an atomic bomb test in September 1954, in order to ascertain whether or not troops could engage in battle in an area immediately after it was hit by an atomic bomb.

A second event that prompted our thinking about crime and punishment in technological society was the revelation that Rik Scarce, a PhD candidate in environmental sociology at Washington

2   MKULTRA activity by the US government "was concerned with the research and development of chemical, biological, and radiological material capable of employment in clandestine operations to control human behavior" (US Senate, 1976:879). The cryptonym MULKTRA encompassed the research and development phase, and the cryptonym MKDELTA denoted the "system for control of the operational employment of such materials." For instance, "Atom 1, 2, 3" was a study in which pigs were fed radioactive food, then were slaughtered and fed to Native Americans in Northern Arizona. Another plan involved creating lakes and reservoirs by setting off atomic bombs (Supkow et al., 1976).

State University, had been incarcerated in Spokane (Washington) County Jail from May until August of 1993 on a charge of contempt of court for refusing to divulge to a federal grand jury the content of confidential interviews he had conducted with, among others, several Earth First! activists as part of his research on the environmental movement (American Sociological Association, 1993: 5). At a time when Earth First! organizers were charging the US Forest Service with destroying old-growth forests in the Pacific Northwest and endangering the survival of the red squirrel atop Mt. Graham in Arizona (*Aleh-zon*, 1991: 10) in order to build a telescope, Scarce's case raised significant questions about the validity of using "subjugated knowledge"[3] (Foucault, 1977) as a basis for legitimate academic inquiry. It also raised questions about the need for researchers to protect their sources of information from the intrusions of government and corporate officials who might be seen as being engaged in white-collar, environmental crime.

The final circumstance that helped to clarify our thoughts on the role of differing concepts of justice in destabilizing modern governments and corporations was the appearance of Cable and Benson's (1993) scholarly article on environmental injustice. This study contends that the emergence of grassroots organizations in the United States is largely due to the failure of state and federal environmental regulatory processes to protect citizens from corporate pollution (see, e.g., Freudenburg and Gramling, 1994). Cable and Benson also suggest that when they do form as a response, grassroots organizations and activists are far less concerned with national environmental policy than with local environmental problems.

Among the more interesting features of Cable and Benson's work is their attempt (1993: 465) at building a "new analytical framework" for viewing the state's environmental regulatory activities, their description of some "patterns" they believe to exist in the formation of grassroots organizations, their discussions of "the strategies used to exert influence on enforcement processes" (1993: 465), and their efforts at distinguishing between an *environmental problem* and a

---

3   Subjugated knowledge refers to unofficial information (sometimes suppressed) that comes from the periphery, rather than the center, of a given power structure.

corporate environmental crime (emphasis theirs) in order to explain the "legitimation crisis" (Habermas, 1975) *generated by pressures placed upon the liberal-democratic state and its regulatory agencies as the latter attempt to respond to environmental difficulties.*

According to Cable and Benson (1993: 465), "the environmental regulatory process often fails to protect citizens from corporate environmental crimes because of the inherent contradictions of the liberal democratic state." In other words, the state is charged with the simultaneous and potentially conflicting tasks of facilitating corporations' economic objectives and providing for the public welfare. Cable and Benson (1993: 467) cite Habermas (1975) and others in contending that the contradictory roles of the state are clearly demonstrated in its actions on environmental issues. The state tends to promote policies that *limit corporate liability* for environmental damages because it must foster capital accumulation and increased economic growth (Cable and Benson, 1993: 468).

Within this general framework, Cable and Benson (1993: 465) assert that citizen-operated grassroots organizations form as a result of actual or perceived environmental problems and begin to "exhibit patterns" in the "strategies used to exert influence on enforcement processes." The coauthors further delineate four stages in the life cycle of these groups. In phase one, residents come to think of themselves as victims of a corporate environmental crime. Phase two involves individual appeals to state regulatory processes, which citizens expect to enforce corporate compliance. In phase three, there is a perception of *environmental injustice*, with citizens becoming increasingly disillusioned with the state and its "seemingly inadequate, often incompetent responses" (Cable and Benson, 1993: 471-473). Phase four concerns the outcome of the "legitimation crisis" (Habermas, 1975) generated democratically by public pressure placed upon the state and its regulatory agencies.

Cable and Benson (1993: 471) note that the phasic order may not follow the above sequence exactly "and that some phases may occur almost simultaneously." More importantly, they argue (Cable and Benson, 1993: 493) that "if collective democratic pressures for environmental reform in a community are successful, the state resolves the legitimacy crisis by enforcing environmental standards *only in that particular case*" (emphasis theirs).

A closer look at Habermas's (1975) legitimation crisis theory indicates that Cable and Benson provide a fairly accurate portrayal of his original contentions while extending the theory to begin to account for the rise of grassroots activism in liberal democracies as a result of increased environmental pollution.

Habermas (1975) wrote of breakdown in state authority when the public withdraws support from officialdom due to its perceptions that government policies and practices are unfair and contradictory. He contends that legitimation problems arise in the West because the state must fulfill the contradictory demands of ensuring capitalist high-technology growth while maintaining mass public support. The former imperative, he believes, requires that the state favor the particular interests of those in control of the means of production; the latter imperative demands that the state act *as if* it represents the interests of all segments of society. Habermas (1975) argues that class interests of the state, which are revealed by its social policies (some of which are mentioned in the present study), work to undermine the mass public support that is necessary to maintain an authentically democratic society. However, Habermas's theory does not track the increasingly direct relationship between economic production, on the one hand, and environmental pollution and the emergence of grassroots, antiregime environmental action, on the other. A more complete treatment can be found in the work of Michael Edelstein (1988), among others.

Taken together, Habermas's (1975) "legitimation crisis" theory and Cable and Benson's (1993) four "stages in the life cycle of grassroots environmental organizations" provide researchers with a useful framework for analyzing interviews with grassroots environmental activists. Specifically, they facilitate determining simultaneously (1) whether these activists reflect the delegitimating dynamic of modern, liberal, and capitalist economies and if so (2) whether they (a) perceive their role as do the experts (Habermas, 1975) and (b) act out their disenchantment with the state in ways described by Cable and Benson (1993).

Scope and Methods

The research plan that developed from these speculations involved interviewing twenty-five nuclear activists in the United

States and Canada to learn about their experiences in organizing small grassroots environmental organizations. The findings were then compared to interviews of a similar group of Western European environmentalists after the Chernobyl nuclear reactor accident. This approach, it was thought, would amplify Habermas's as well as Cable and Benson's work bilaterally. First, it would *reflect legitimation crisis in contemporary societies manifested in the form of environmental whistle-blowing, mass social discontent, and proposals for social reform in (non) democratic polities.* Second, it would *provide researchers with a richer understanding of real-world connections among an increasing array of "normal" technological accidents globally* (Perrow, 1984) *and the delegitimation of all modern growth economies, no matter their political-economic ideology.*

Accordingly, the author set out to compare relevant materials from his ongoing, in-depth interviews of North American activists, with Dr. Mark Reader's set of taped interviews of grassroots European environmentalists and political decision-makers, recorded in Europe during July-August 1986, after the Chernobyl disaster. This promised to provide a way to test some of Cable and Benson's (1993: 465) and Habermas's hypotheses and to examine the role that technological catastrophe played in delegitimating the Soviet regime and the Japanese government after Fukushima.

The plan that emerged while measuring regime disaffection among local environmentalists was to focus on the underlying theme of *environmental injustice* as identified by grassroots leaders and to look at the critical moment in the delegitimation process when an *environmental problem* is redefined by sociologists as an *institutional crime.* In so doing, the authors hoped to gain sociological insight into the contextual meaning of the term *legitimation crisis,* to describe how and when an authority crisis in the modern state is perceived by those involved, and to learn which of Cable and Benson's major assertions might be confirmed by our data.

In addition to using interview data, Dr. Reader and I examined a wealth of published material on the way(s) that citizens in local communities respond to radiation incidents, as well as a number of discussions of potential "environmental crimes" in scholarly journals, magazines, newspapers, and institute reports. We also looked at changes in the word *crime* as used by environmental activists and decided to employ some previously published data (Edelstein, 1988; Mander, 1991; Reader et al., 1980) on the way in which technological disasters make explicit many of the hidden social costs of contradictions built into the operation of high technologies.

Respondents were interviewed in-depth as environmental activists (Monroe, 1991) or "altruists" (Oliner and Oliner, 1988), without asking them any questions about environmental crime or a possible legitimation crisis for the state. The interviews were then analyzed inductively for specific incidents and concomitant community reactions that implied a possible legitimation crisis, without the researcher projecting any particular theoretical framework onto the data. All respondents were asked the same set of open-ended questions: a brief history of their personal involvement with the environmental problem, any psychosocial effects of the problem either upon them or the community at large, opinions regarding local and national government in relation to the environmental problem, obstacles (if any) encountered in attempting to alleviate the problem, agencies and/or individuals that were helpful, successes, failures, or disappointments experienced during grassroots organizing, and future plans for dealing with the problem.

Of the twenty-five respondents from the United States and Canada included in the present study, all were interviewed on several occasions, with at least one tape-recorded session for each respondent. The interviews extended from a minimum of 2 hours to a maximum of 6 hours or more. Arranging for these interviews involved attendance at various meetings, public hearings, and other grassroots events. Twenty-four additional environmentalists were interviewed but not included in the present study because they had not challenged the system such that they were labeled "leaders" in any local environmental movement. Direct verbal or written contact with either polluters or agency officials is considered by some a basic criterion for being considered a grassroots activist organizer (Cable and Benson, 1993: 468-469). Not included in this analysis are data from three interviewees in the United States and Canada who were plaintiffs in pending lawsuits. Although no other respondents requested anonymity, fictitious first names were used throughout to protect respondents from unwanted notoriety. Similar anonymity was afforded to the European post-Chernobyl interviewees for much the same reason.

In the remaining sections of this chapter, we are going to present a full discussion of environmental crime and legitimation crisis theory as related to the goals of the present research, the data analysis, and some reflections on the implications of the study for social scientists and for the future of democracy in an increasingly technological age.

Environmental Crime and the US Legitimation Crisis

In spite of many recent media revelations concerning the US governmental secrecy and deception, especially in connection with radioactive and chemical contamination at US nuclear weapons plants (see, e.g., Freudenburg and Youn, 1993), it is worth noting how seldom the term *environmental crime* is used in connection with state and federal regulatory agencies. When the term is used, it is regarded in a legal—rather than a moral or ethical—sense. Cable and Benson (1993: 465) argue only that "environmental pollution resulting from a corporation's violations of environmental law constitutes corporate environmental crime." Other sociologists (Williams and McShane, 1994) contend that although state crimes are committed by all governments, practical solutions to such criminal activity are not found readily. For instance, in the 1940s and 1950s, massive doses of radioactive iodine-131 were deliberately released across the Pacific Northwest from the Hanford Nuclear Reservation in Washington State (Cobb, 1989; D'Antonio, 1994; Gallo, 1993). This prompted local Washington farmer, Tom Bailie, to assert: "We are victims of this mismanagement," "I really think someone should to go jail for manslaughter" (Cobb, 1989: 433), and "I think someone, maybe even the President, ought to apologize" (D'Antonio, 1994).

Similarly, government environmental crime has been *implied* in connection with both the Savannah River and Fernald nuclear weapons plants (Schneider, 1988a, 1988b). The Savannah River plant in South Carolina has experienced numerous reactor incidents that were kept from the public for up to 31 years (Gould and Goldman, 1990). Physicists have termed these events among the most severe ever documented at American nuclear plants. Several additional incidents at the Fernald plant near Cincinnati, Ohio, also seem to suggest criminal activity (CBS News, 1991). These include workers contaminated with hydrofluoric acid and uranium oxide dust, radioactive contamination of private water wells near the plant, ignorance of environmental laws and regulations on the part of DOE contractors, repeated denials of the presence of thorium at Fernald, after a DOE safety appraisal had acknowledged its presence about 1½ years earlier (USDOE, 1989: B-7), and a letter to the contractor at Fernald from a consultant at Battelle/Pacific Northwest Laboratories, warning that a proposed employee picnic at Fernald was "an extremely poor idea" because even the plant's "clean zone" was contaminated (Hardert, 1993: 131-134). Yet in spite of these and other questionable environmental activities involving both corporate and government environmental actors, the term *crime* is encountered rarely in media descriptions of such bureaucratic or institutional behavior whether public or private.

However, the situation at Rocky Flats nuclear plant near Denver is somewhat different (*PBS News*, 1993). In this case, citizens impaneled on the grand jury perceived both corporate and regulatory environmental crime, and spoke in those terms. In fact, the Colorado grand jury wrote a report accusing the DOE of conspiring with their contractor, Rockwell, to commit and hide a number of environmental crimes (McKinley and Balkany, 2004). The report described Rocky Flats as "an ongoing criminal enterprise," *allowed to operate with the complicity of government and corporate employees* (emphasis ours) who "have breached the public's trust by engaging in a campaign of distraction, deception, and dishonesty" (Abas, 1992: 16). The grand jurors then submitted their report to the US District Judge Sherman Finesilver and expected him to make the report public (McKinley and Balkany, 2004). To date, the document has not been released, despite federal law that permits the judge to release it, as long as certain legal requirements are met. Meanwhile, the federal legal system has pressured the jurors to remain silent or face possible indictment for divulging information from grand jury deliberations to the public. To complicate matters, the grand jury also proposed indictments against both Rockwell and DOE employees, which the US Attorney

Michel Norton refused to sign "for lack of evidence," rendering the indictments invalid (Abas, 1992: 15).

Since June 1992, the Subcommittee on Investigations and Oversight, chaired by Congressman Howard Wolpe of Michigan, has been reviewing the settlement which concluded government investigation and prosecution for environmental crimes of Rockwell, Inc., at the DOE's Rocky Flats nuclear weapons facility. A cover letter attached to the Wolpe report (1993: 1-2) and directed to the subcommittee chair underscores several important findings. First, the investigation revealed a "very troubling lack of public accountability in the federal Government." Reportedly, serious environmental crimes were committed, but no individuals were held accountable (Wolpe, 1993: 1). Instead, the crimes were attributed to a reified (abstract) nuclear "culture" at DOE, not to the actions of specific individuals. Second, it was noted that federal prosecutors relinquished the truth in negotiations with Rockwell. "By entering into a plea agreement with Rockwell, the prosecutors bargained away the right to fully and accurately inform the American people and the Congress about the conditions, activities, and crimes at the Rocky Flats facility" (Wolpe, 1993: 2). Wolpe (1993: 2) added, "And these conditions are not unique to Rocky Flats. They can be found throughout the DOE complex." Third, the report indicated sympathy for the Rocky Flats jury that Wolpe (1993: 2) said, "were so offended by the plea agreement with Rockwell that they have placed themselves in legal jeopardy by publicly discussing the settlement."

Under the plea agreement, Rockwell pled guilty to ten criminal counts under two environmental laws: four felony counts under the Resource Conservation and Recovery Act, in addition to one felony count and five misdemeanors under the Clean Water Act. The contractor paid a fine of $18.5 million—of which $16.5 million went to the federal government and $2 million to the State of Colorado (Wolpe, 1993: 29). This is the largest environmental fine ever levied, after that in the *Exxon Valdez* case. However, Wolpe (1993: 29) characterized the *Exxon Valdez* incident as "more of a case of unforgivable negligence, whereas the individuals at Rocky Flats intentionally violated laws for prolonged periods of time."

In addition to suggesting that the US government and private corporations, as well as individual persons, have committed various environmental crimes, the Wolpe's report is important for the present analysis, in that it demonstrates two potential weaknesses in Cable and Benson's (1993) study: their lack of emphasis on possible regulatory environmental crimes as a contributory source of citizen disaffection with the authorities (see, e.g., Tsoukalas, 1994) and a tendency to de-emphasize government-initiated environmental policies as major wellsprings of institutional crime in the United States. Equally important, the Wolpe's report sharpens the common sense perception that there is a world of difference between referring to an action by a government, one of its regulatory agencies, or a corporation, as either a "problem" at one extreme or a "crime" or "legitimation crisis" at the other. The disparity between the uses of these words may serve as an indicator of the extent to which any particular individual or grassroots social organization has become alienated from the regime, a point obscured by Cable and Benson and by Habermas in their discussions of "legitimation crisis." We return to this concern later.

We now turn to analysis of the interviews with grassroots environmental leaders in order to illustrate the practical and theoretical importance of placing this perspective on environmental crime within a broader institutional and ethical context.

Data Analysis: the United States and Canada

The data analysis of interviews with nuclear activists focuses on Cable and Benson's (1993) "four stages in the emergence of grassroots organizations" in the United States, in the context of a possible ongoing "legitimation crisis" (Habermas, 1975) within advanced technological society and its various regulatory agencies. Published accounts of both corporate and possible regulatory environmental crime discussed in the previous section suggest that US regulatory agencies are already in a state of crisis. Further analysis of the original interview data in this study may or may not support that interpretation.

Cable and Benson's (1993) four stages are difficult to test directly because (1) most of our data are qualitative, (2) the actual order of stages may not follow exactly the sequence noted in their article, and (3) some phases may occur simultaneously (Cable and Benson, 1993:

471). Nevertheless, analysis of interview data indicates that nuclear respondents in the United States were slow to realize that a *corporate crime* might have occurred in their situation and rather quick to define their circumstance as an *environmental problem* existing in the community. So prevalent was this finding that we suggest that Cable and Benson either redefine phase one (i.e., perception as victims) or move it lower in the ordering of environmental-group life-cycle stages. Phase three, the perception of environmental injustice, seems to overlap phase one since most respondents indicated they perceived some degree of environmental injustice early in the process. Nevertheless, phase two individual appeals to state/regulatory processes appeared early in the interview data, as Cable and Benson surmised, but almost simultaneously with phase three, that is, the perception of environmental injustice in the sense of perceiving that their environmental problem is left unaddressed by state agencies. This analytical difficulty is consistent with Cable and Benson's assertion that some stages in the formation of grassroots environmental organizations occur simultaneously. However, it seems preferable to view these phases as *factors* involved in a *process*, rather than as true evolutionary stages.

Nuclear Activism

Some examples from the nuclear activist interviews are instructive in understanding both the complexity of the phase-ordering problem noted above and the issue of potential state legitimation crisis. Lisa Crawford, president of FRESH, the grassroots organization located near the Fernald nuclear weapons facility that reportedly contaminated its workers and the surrounding community for some 38 years (Barton, 1994: A1, A5), describes her group and herself as "essentially nonnuclear rather than antinuclear" in orientation. During numerous grassroots meetings and one 6-hour interview, she never used the terms *crime* or *criminal activity*, so phase one, as described in Cable and Benson (1993), seems to be missing in the evolution of this particular organization. Nevertheless, Lisa and other FRESH members do *imply* possible criminal activity on the part of the DOE and one of its earlier contractors in much of what they say about possible deception and cover-ups.

Chronologically speaking, with the exception of having to reword Cable and Benson's (1993) phase one terminology by replacing the term *corporate crime*[4] with the phrase *environmental problem*, the development of Lisa's organization does parallel their four life-cycle stages for grassroots organizations fairly closely. Phase one,—the discovery of excess levels of uranium in three private (off-site) water wells—occurred in the winter of 1984. By the spring of 1985, Lisa began to appeal to state and federal regulatory agencies (i.e., phase two).

". . . DOE did not have a site office at that time so you had to talk to people in Oak Ridge (National Laboratory), which was becoming very expensive and very frustrating. The local contractor, National Lead of Ohio, would not return my phone calls, would not talk to me, would not give me copies of letters. . . . And it was like I didn't have any rights at all. Then I began to call the Ohio EPA and the Ohio Department of Health. You get an education real fast."

Later, Lisa began to perceive more in the way of environmental injustice (phase three):

> "The big time was in September of 1988. . . . That's when the lawsuit was becoming hot and heavy, and that's when we exchanged interrogatories with their lawyers . . . The question was asked 'Did you (NLO and DOE) knowingly and willingly pollute the environment?' And their answer was: 'Yes, we did. But, there is nothing you can do about it, because we fall under the guise of national security.' And the second question was 'What is a safe level of radiation?' And their answer was: 'None. There is none.' And that caused a fervor you would not believe."

4   Leaders of small grassroots environmental organizations do not tend to use terms such as *corporate crime* until or unless they are involved in toxic tort litigation. This reflects their uncertainty concerning exactly what constitutes an environmental crime from a legal point of view (Sharkansky, 2000:35-52).

Phase four relates to the result of increased democratic pressure. Cable and Benson (1993: 472) explain that if the grassroots environmental group is successful, the state resolves the legitimation crisis by enforcing environmental standards. Since Lisa and her group are one of the few grassroots organizations ever to have won a major class-action lawsuit against the DOE and one of its contractors (Hardert, 1993: 137-138), we could say their group was successful. Still, certain corporate infractions continue at the weapons plant and environmental problems persist.

More important than the sequencing problems in Cable and Benson's (1993) stages are the questions of environmental crime and legitimation crisis considered within the context of the organizational-development phases discussed earlier. At a minimum, phase two through four of Cable and Benson's typology appears to be valid for Lisa's group and for most other nuclear organizations in our interview data.

Another nuclear interview was with Don Hancock, the director of an organization that is opposed to the WIPP near Carlsbad, New Mexico. The purpose of WIPP is to provide permanent storage of low-level and intermediate-level nuclear waste generated primarily by military nuclear reactors. Don expressed what sounds like phase one perceptions: "There have always been problems with the facility," and "The more we have found out about WIPP, the worse the site seems to be." However, unlike the phase one assertion claims in Cable and Benson (1993), Hancock makes no mention of any corporate environmental crime and refers only to the existence of a number of environmental problems. This is not to say that Don lacked critical thinking skills regarding a possible legitimation crisis connected with the WIPP project. Rather, he seemed unwilling to reach any conclusive judgments based on his own experience. For instance, regarding the DOE, he said,

> ". . . the Department has no credibility, not only with WIPP, but you can look at Yucca Mountain (the proposed high level, nuclear waste repository in Nevada), and you can look at the second-round sites they consider. You can look at all their facilities, whether it's Idaho (Idaho National Engineering Laboratory near Idaho Falls),

Fernald in Ohio, Savannah River in South Carolina, Oak Ridge in Tennessee, Rocky Flats in Colorado, or Hanford in Washington State. I mean *any* (emphasis his) of the DOE facilities. DOE has no credibility. They have a record of contaminating facilities, of lying to the public, of misrepresenting things to the public. So I have said for a number of years, if we want to solve the nuclear waste problem in this country, the Department of Energy has to be taken out of it."

Note that the term *crime* does not appear in Don's statement, but taken as a whole, he certainly *implies* the type of duplicity contained in Sutherland's (1983) conceptualization of white-collar crime, that is, as criminal violation of public trust.

Regarding Cable and Benson's (1993: 472) phase four concern for "the legitimacy crisis generated by democratic pressures," Hancock sees some success in the battle to establish definite criteria for the establishment of all waste facilities. However, he also laments that "it is going to take a long time to develop solutions" and that "we haven't been able to kill WIPP completely." In response to Cable and Benson's phase four assertions concerning a possible legitimacy crisis for the DOE at WIPP, one may wonder how many American citizens are even aware of the DOE's role in creating environmental problems.

Within the nuclear interviews, most of the twenty-five North American respondents provided information freely regarding their grassroots work, the environmental *concerns* that led to it (phase two), and the disillusionment that set in (phase three) when the regulatory process failed them. The remaining interviewee—Don Hancock—assumed a more detached, "scholarly," and "analytical" position in tending not to personalize his experience during the interview, except for his comments about the DOE.

By way of contrast, another respondent did suggest that he and many other peace and antinuclear power activists experienced a more fundamental break with regime values. In phase four discussion of "the outcome of increased democratic pressure," "Harry"—a professor and sponsor of various student-environmental organizations—characterized grassroots environmental leaders in the following way:

"I think these quiet heroes . . . (have) all had to sacrifice something to do what they're doing: loss of job, loss of reputation, loss of health. But, rather than doing violence to others, they take it on themselves and simply stand in the situations of the traditional civil disobedient or Camus's rebel, where you say 'No' to injustice and 'Yes' to life."

And in a statement hinting at some fundamental changes in his self-concept that resulted from his own local grassroots antinuclear activism, Harry confided,

"You know, I've never wanted to be arrested. I never wanted or imagined I would be doing what I'm doing, but I can't imagine doing anything else. I know that if I've got the physical capacity, when the next set of problems comes along, reluctantly, I'll have to speak out on them, and it's going to be the same thing . . . Whatever I've accomplished, I have accomplished without giving up my humanity. In fact, I think I've deepened my humanity."

Cable and Benson's (1993) analysis, as well as our interviews with grassroots environmentalists, tends to support the general observation that the authorities in liberal, capitalist economies have been able to use the culturally shared belief in the existence of democracy to prevent the emergence of legitimation problems potentially fatal to their rule and that with few exceptions, local activists in both the United States and Canada have been willing to accept the regime's view that if justice is denied in one area of the polity, it will be corrected in another. Thus, as our interviews both in the United States and Western Europe indicate, even when they believe that they or their loved ones have been harmed physically by the actions of either their governments or the modern corporation, grassroots environmental activists have sought neither the dissolution of the state nor the dominant economic paradigm. What they settled for, instead, are civil, usually monetary, penalties for perceived government or corporate wrongdoing and symbolic punishments of *individuals* whom they hold responsible for what they consider criminal acts, again defined in monetary terms, as, for example, in the case of the Rocky Flats nuclear plant near Denver (Wolpe, 1993).

Nevertheless, our interviews also reveal that insofar as regime disaffection is experienced by environmental activists in the United States, it is often first encountered in their exposure to the workings of government regulatory agencies as the latter attempt to respond to local concerns about radiation and chemical/pesticide pollution. It is in these encounters that the process of delegitimation may sometimes escalate from a low-level legitimating *crisis* into a full-scale legitimating *confrontation* between the public and the authorities. For instance, it is generally agreed that the use of "stun guns" by sheriff's department officers against grassroots peace and environment organizers participating in a hazardous waste facility hearing was decisive in persuading the state of Arizona to reverse a decision to locate a hazardous waste facility near the community of Mobile, Arizona (Clifford, 1993: 67-69).

Data Analysis: Post-Chernobyl Interviews

Despite the apparent lesson taught by American interviewees, limited grassroots response to perceived environmental crimes, allegedly committed by those in authority, may not be universal. Our own data and other published accounts of interviews with European grassroots environmental activists in the post-Chernobyl period indicate that *technological disaster* can present the powerful in any polity with a series of potentially insoluble governing problems, as seemingly happened in the former Communist Bloc after the world's most severe industrial calamity (Hawkes, 1986). Such accidents apparently reveal to potential grassroots environmental activists the often-hidden *personal* and *structural* contradictions, which are associated with many of the techniques and tools that constitute industrial civilization (Edelstein, 1988; Mander, 1991; Mumford, 1967). Thus, they convince a number of previously quiescent citizens to take direct action to protect themselves from further destructive decisions of the technological regime (Reader, 1983).

Analysis of our data, collected during a seven-nation fact-finding tour of Western Europe and the Nordic nations 3 months after Chernobyl, in addition to continuing analysis of various scholarly and popular Russian sources, reveals a pattern of widespread citizen awareness of their vulnerability to government-sponsored technologies, their dependency upon elites for radiation information vital to their lives (Flavin, 1987), and the belief that authorities were lying about the incident's seriousness. Also apparent in the aftermath of the disaster were grassroots attempts to secure alternative sources of reliable radiation information, complete with popular demands for dosimeters (radiation measuring devices), and formation of community-based food-information networks. In the former Communist Bloc, under the ever-present threat of radiation poisoning, this included discarding previous technological illusions in favor of a view of the Chernobyl disaster as a metaphor for everything wrong in Soviet communist society. Subsequent evidence suggests that as a result of Chernobyl, large numbers of Eastern Europeans concluded that communist authorities were engaged in criminal acts in an ethical rather than merely a legal sense of the term and that each person was morally obligated to combat the system of state terrorism, if only to survive.

Western Europe

Uncertainty and fear were expressed throughout the European continent immediately following the Chernobyl catastrophe, as winds and radiation-bearing clouds showered their deadly poisons from the stricken Soviet nuclear reactor around the earth. Early dispatches from the disaster scene reported the evacuation of 135,000 persons from an 18-mile zone around the atomic city of Pripyat in the weeks immediately following the fire in and explosion of Unit. 4 of the Wormwood plant. Thousands of Kiev schoolchildren, living some 70 miles to the southeast, were hurriedly sent off to various parts of the Soviet Union for early summer vacation, far from the burning reactor.

In early May 1986, the Danish mother of a colleague reported:

> ". . . There is no place to hide from the radioactive clouds. Winds keep blowing hither and thither over Europe from Kiev's smoldering atomic reactor. What a scare! More than ever, we are pressing Sweden to shut down their reactors, only 230 km from Copenhagen, right

across from Kronborg castle (Hamlet's home)—even if they are much safer built than the Russians' are. . . . Yes, the European countries did send out warnings but mostly reassuring messages depending on how heavy each of them have invested in and are depending on the nuclear power, not wanting to rouse public opinion against them. Since you have heard all about it and seen the hearings on it on your TV, I will say no more except that we have no reactors ourselves but are surrounded with many and especially the ones in East Germany, built on the Russian model. Thus a big cause of worry for the whole of Europe. Strangely enough—the winds that gave us, and still do, the unusual warm sunny spring come from the southeast, the very same bringing the air laden with death by radioactive particles. But at the moment a stronger current blows them from Kiev over Turkey and the Balkan lands. Progress has its price, difficult to estimate (Vognsen, 1986)."

As memorable as these images are, they do not include the additional hundreds of thousands of Soviet citizens relocated from contaminated villages in Ukraine, Belarus, and Russia in the years since Chernobyl, the thousands of soldiers and workers from around the Former Soviet Union rushed into the region to clean up the damage, nor those still living in the newly independent, former Soviet republics whose health was jeopardized by the accident. For example, a 1991 study found that 1.8 million people, including 250,000 children, were still living in areas contaminated by the accident (Massik, 1991: 205). Moreover, in October 1992, then President Boris Yelstin, of Russia, released an environmental/public health report indicating that at least 2.3 million Russians were still living in areas polluted by the Chernobyl and other industrial wastelands (*Arizona Republic*, 1992: A7).

Popular concern about the reactor's potential radiation hazards for everyday life was still evident throughout Western Europe as this study's seven-nation fact-finding tour of the sociopolitical impact of Chernobyl began 10 weeks after the accident. Telephone switchboards at the WISE, in Amsterdam, continued to respond to callers asking for information about the relative safety of eating locally produced legumes, and a clerk in an Oslo indoor market steered this study's interviewers past Norwegian cheese suspected of contamination in favor of "safer" imported Swiss Ementhaler.

Eastern Europe

The denial option noted earlier was not available to inhabitants of Eastern Europe, however. The fire and explosion at the Pripyat reactor impacted them with the psychological forces of an atomic bomb, erasing whatever emotional and ideological distance they had previously established between themselves and their nuclear nightmares. Almost overnight, ordinary people throughout the Communist Bloc began to think of themselves as nuclear victims and survivors, and insofar as they did, they began to take survival into their own hands. Echoing the thoughts of many, one commentator (Shaw, 1992: 62) observed,

> "For everyone who participated, directly or indirectly, in the tragedy of Chernobyl . . . time seems to have split into two unequal parts; before April 26, 1986, and after (as one person after another stepped from a pre-holocaust era into) an unknown epoch which demanded a fundamental restructuring of their thought."

Realizing that both she and her neighbors were likely victims of the disaster, survivor Liubova Oleksandrivna Kovalevska, a newspaper writer/author, recalls (Shcherbak, 1989: 69),

> "I took a bath, I ran the water and I relieved myself by weeping. And I wept at a table. I felt so much pain for people, for the lack of truth. The newspapers were writing lies. Perhaps it was the first time I had come close up against this . . . To know the real essence of things and to read such bravura articles. It was a terrible shock and deeply upset me."

As the dimensions of the Chernobyl accident became more evident, those most immediately affected by it concluded that communist party officials not only had mishandled events leading up to the catastrophe but subsequently had lied to them about the gravity of their situation. Some dated their post-Chernobyl resistance against communist rule to the official resettlement of unsuspecting accident victims from the 10-km zone nearest the stricken plant, beginning on April 27. They condemned party leaders (Shcherbak, 1989; Voznesenskaya, 1987) for fleeing the disaster scene, to putting up a business-as-usual façade in the wake of the mishap, for not preparing the evacuees for a prolonged exile from their homes, for separating parents from children for lengthy periods of time and relocating them at distant and unfamiliar places, for the poor housing accommodations and sometimes hostile reception afforded those they relocated, and finally, for deliberately failing to inform those most at risk of the accident's health hazards. Others came to resent the authorities for the abortions they had to undergo, often by the same medical personnel they held responsible for not alerting them to the perils posed by the accident earlier.

More than anything else that strained relationships between Eastern Europeans and communist officials to the breaking point, however, was the authorities' decision to hold annual May Day celebrations 5 days after the catastrophe, having previously and secretly evacuated their own children from highly contaminated areas. Thus, in identifying *the event* that had motivated them to seek political independence from Moscow in the years following the accident, two high-ranking Ukrainian Green World environmental activists (Mishchenko and Panov, 1991) recalled bitterly how local party officials from Kiev had begun furtive relocation of their own children in the immediate aftermath of the accident, but in public, they "denied that anything unusual had happened (so that on May 1, 1986, they were able to march) tens of thousands (of innocent young people through an environment) saturated with radioactive poisons to celebrate the glories of the Communist reign."

Given the realization that they and their children had been betrayed by those same authorities they customarily depended on for their daily existence, many people began to reject all official definitions of their reality. This initiated direct opposition to the communist regime, something citizens had been unwilling and unable to do while radiation contamination had remained only a psychological threat, as it had throughout the whole of the Cold War period, rather than a real physical presence in their lives. By May 7, more than a week before Premier Gorbachev appeared on national television to discuss the mishap, members of the Moscow Trust group (WISE, 1986) were risking police arrest in order to gather hard-to-find bits of information about the disaster and to demand an immediate halt to the Soviet Union's nuclear power program because of "the inherent dangers of the so-called peaceful applications of nuclear energy."

This coupling of antiregime and antinuclear power sentiment swept across the Soviet bloc, with critics of communist government as far west as the former GDR indicting governing scientific and political elites in the United States, the Soviet Union, and their own country for using their monopoly on radiation information to "tranquilize" public opinion about the twin dangers of nuclear energy and the Chernobyl debacle.

As apparently self-destructive as the authorities' actions were, they nevertheless possessed a certain logic. First, as in the aftermath of technological disaster experienced elsewhere around the world, Soviet officialdom had to walk a fine line between persuading at-risk populations in contaminated areas that Chernobyl presented some danger to their health and safety, but not enough to warrant panic (Edelstein, 1988). This helps explain why local communist party functionaries acted so matter-of-factly in evacuating survivors from the Pripyat disaster zone, failing to prepare soon-to-be homeless inhabitants adequately for major disruptions in their lives (Shcherbak, 1989). It also accounts for the dramatic loss in government authority in the minds of many ordinary Soviet citizens—particularly in the Ukraine, Byelorussia, and Moldavia—as the "aftershocks of Chernobyl" continued to be felt during the next several years and as it became known that the tragedy was far more devastating than authorities had led the public to believe initially.

"After the accident, the people of my country waited for 2 weeks for Gorbachev to face the problem," sculptor Woloymjir Iwanow, president of the Ukrainian Greens, later complained to the Spanish newspaper, *El Independiente* (Feinstein, 1992: 611).

"But Gorbachev did nothing for us, on the contrary, the central government decided to cover up the consequences of the accident, to the point that today, we have half a million children suffering from sickness provoked by radioactivity, and the central government of Gorbachev still goes on not recognizing them as affected by Chernobyl."

Complicating Moscow's ability to respond to the disaster effectively was years of secretive, centralized, and punitive communist rule. Bureaucratic decision-making guaranteed that reliable information about the accident could not and would not be transmitted quickly or accurately enough through the party's intricate chain of command to enable decisive, on-site medical action in the days immediately following the breakdown. Further, the Kremlin's long-standing practice of cloaking even the most trivial of its decisions in bureaucratic obfuscation assured that Gorbachev's *glasnost* policy, articulated less than a month earlier at the 27th Congress of the Communist Party, would have little impact on the way officials reacted to the accident and would actually complicate the Russian leader's efforts to consolidate his political power (Jones and Woodbury, 1986).

Given these structural problems, lesser party leaders throughout the Western Soviet republics withheld information from Moscow about the emergency's character for as long as they dared, fearing they would be punished for allowing the calamity to occur at all (Shaw, 1992). At the same time, Kremlin decision-makers tied themselves up in administrative knots battling over the relative merits of applying the new *openness* policy to the mishap (Ra'anan, 1986: 249). Accordingly, it was not until May 2, 6 days after the accident started, that any senior government officials visited the disaster zone (Ra'anan, 1986: 253-254) and not until May 6 that the Kremlin began to address the Soviet people's health and safety concerns about the misfortune officially.

What followed was Gorbachev's curious and (for the regimes as well as for his own political authority) tragic misreading of Chernobyl's impact on the everyday lives of citizens throughout the Communist Bloc. For some unknown reason, the new Soviet leader kept insisting publicly that the central lesson of Chernobyl was the unacceptability of nuclear war. Rather than acknowledging just how terrifying the government's electricity-producing nuclear reactors had suddenly become, he argued that a nuclear arms accord with the United States was an essential consequence of the accident (Marples, 1988). By echoing his analysis, top-level officials lost the opportunity to rally the peoples of Eastern Europe in common cause against the invisible and menacing radiation threat and squandered their remaining political capital among rank-and-file communist party faithful as well.

"Surely you must understand that my interest at the moment isn't in the supposed horrors of a third world war," Julia Voznesenskaya's semi-autobiographical heroine (1987: 69) cries out as she reaches desperately for missing family members at Chernobyl immediately after the catastrophe.

> "(W)hat I'm worried about is the condition of people irradiated now, in peace-time. You don't have to propagandize me about peace and disarmament. I'm a communist myself . . . I'm interested in . . . what's happening to those irradiated people."

Faced with a widening gap between its and the public's perception of the accident's significance, the Gorbachev leadership did what elites elsewhere have done repeatedly, whenever a prized technology has been cut out from under them: it minimized the health and safety dangers posed by the catastrophe, held individual persons rather than an apparently effective technological system responsible for the reactor's malfunction, blamed Chernobyl's victims for contributing to their own victimization, and, these steps failing, eventually tried to erase the debacle from people's memories by declaring the Pripyat disaster zone to be a tourist attraction.

Thus, even as the scientific director of the disaster zone was reporting that more than seven thousand persons had lost their lives as a result of the breakdown, Moscow was still asserting that only thirty-two persons had died in the accident, vilifying a handful of reactor operators and managers for either causing or contributing pivotally to the failure. Moscow also suppressed information to the effect that as early as 7 years prior to the meltdown (February 1979), the KGB had warned the Central Committee of the Soviet Union secretly of serious "design deviations and violations of construction" that "could lead to mishaps and accidents" at the Chernobyl facility (NYT 6/15/92:A7). It also supported a highly controversial IAEA study that accused many supposed victims of the tragedy of suffering from severe "radiophobia," that is, an irrational fear of radiation contamination (*Washington Post* National Weekly Edition, 1991: 39).

As both the people and a progressively more pragmatic local leadership produced by the accident realized "that their lives did not matter to the state" (Feinstein, 1992: 611), ethnic, nationalist, and class divisions spread throughout the republics (*New York Times*, 1990), reaching such a fever pitch by December 1991 that members of the newly established Ukrainian parliament were demanding that Gorbachev himself be brought to trial for systematically obscuring the human as well as ecological costs of the meltdown (*New York Times*, 1991: A10). Equally significant, the widespread perception of systemic communist incompetency at all levels of government spurred on the anti-regime activities of a broad-based, decentralized, grassroots environmental movement throughout the Soviet Union.

What had gone wrong with the government strategy which, until Chernobyl, had proven so serviceable for other political regimes struggling to regain their damaged credibility in the aftermath of earlier technological breakdowns in the global oil, chemical, and atomic industries? In retrospect, the unprecedented scale, duration, and uniqueness of Chernobyl produced a number of problems which no government could hope to resolve.

First, the *global* radiation fallout from the accident insured that Soviet authorities would be unable to contain information about the failure and the responses of other governments and people to it. As a result, they were never able to control the definition of either the disaster's causes or the consequences. Initially, the incident was detected and reported to the world by Swedish authorities. Thus, from the outset, this created a situation in which the Soviet people relied on non-Soviet sources for vital information. Indeed, many Soviet citizens first learned of the problem by listening to then-banned foreign radio reports emanating from the West, ham radio operators inside the Communist Bloc, international telephone calls from concerned relatives, and word-of-mouth rumors, none of which were monitored by communist officials. In order to combat the resulting erosion of its authority and to convince the populace of the sincerity of its newly pledged "openness," Moscow moved to implement Gorbachev's *glasnost* policies swiftly, *except in those critical situations involving information about atomic and other energy sources*. In so doing, the government triggered a widespread grassroots environmental campaign bent on closing all existing nuclear reactors in the Soviet Union.

Second, Chernobyl quickly became an incident without closure, persuading more and more citizens that the authorities were betraying them despite official protestations to the contrary. Each post-meltdown report brought additional information about problems of new and potential human fatalities generated by the Soviet nuclear industry: contaminated villages, fields, and crops forced exoduses, birth defects, and previous nuclear accidents and cover-ups at Chernobyl and elsewhere in the Soviet nuclear program. All this was taken by the public as fresh evidence of the communist authorities' treacherous unwillingness and continuing inability to guarantee the people's most pressing health and safety needs.

Finally, all available evidence suggests that, from the very beginning, both the Soviet leadership and the public at large associated Chernobyl with grotesque death and thermonuclear extinction, and they reacted accordingly. One must remember that the catastrophe took place in the midst of the Reagan administration's demonizing pseudo-Messianic policies that brought millions of people into the streets of the world's capitals in protest against the prospect of thermonuclear war and prompted some of the world's most renowned physical and biological scientists to endorse the "nuclear winter" thesis (Turco et al., 1984). That thesis predicted the actual end of humanity in the event of a limited thermonuclear exchange between the United States and USSR.

Consequently, images of Armageddon, Hiroshima, and Nagasaki, as well as the Holocaust, became familiar ingredients in postaccident Soviet films, writing, music and art (Marples, 1988), and painting produced by Soviet children displayed in a post-Chernobyl London art show years later. In addition, there was the immediate association of word *Chernobyl* (which means *wormwood* in Russia) with Gothic images of death, dark prophecy, bitterness, and bright hopes gone awry. This resonates with Voznesenskaya's translation of Revelation 8:10-11 in the opening passages of her passionate, personal account of the tragedy (1987):

> "And the third angel sounded, and there fell a great star from heaven, burning as if it were a lamp, and it fell upon the third part of the rivers, and upon the fountains of the waters;
> And the name of the star is called Wormwood; and the third part of the waters became wormwood; and many men died in the waters, because they were made bitter."

This widespread popular encounter with the abyss had two major effects on the Soviet regime's legitimacy in the post-Chernobyl period. On the one hand, it blinded Gorbachev and his closest associates to the real, insoluble dilemmas posed by nuclear power development in the USSR and paralyzed them with respect to organizing the Soviet peoples in common cause against the dangers posed by the meltdown. On the other hand, it created unbearable psychological anguish among former Gorbachev supporters (like Iurii Shcherbak, who was to help found the populist environmental organization, Green World, and eventually become a member of an independent Ukrainian parliament), who soon came to realize the radical character of all nuclear technology, as well as the need to redefine their concepts of self and society, and to take direct, uncompromising action against a regime whose excesses they had tolerated for half a century.

In the end, the so-called "peaceful" atom had proven as politically and psychologically ungovernable for the authorities as the atomic bomb. Officialdom had not protected, and could not protect, the Soviet people from psychic devastation. The authorities had not realized that Chernobyl's slowly widening destructiveness would serve as a constant reminder of the government's role as primary author of terror in an Atomic Age. Ironically, due to their choice of the nuclear power alternative to fulfill their high-technology energy needs, along with the "normal accidents" (Perrow, 1984) to which atomic energy is prone, Soviet officialdom had prepared its own demise.

Crisis of Authority at Fukushima

Regarding Fukushima Daiichi, the Japanese government withheld information about the full consequences of its March 12, 2011 nuclear electric disaster from its own people and from the United States. An independent report by the private Rebuild Japan Initiative Foundation indicates a great deal of confusion during the days immediately following the accident. The report says the US government was frustrated by the scattered information provided by Japan and was skeptical about its truth.

The Japanese government announced in December 2011 that three melted reactors at the Fukushima plant had basically stabilized and that radiation releases had dropped. But the Japanese government did not mention that it would take decades to fully decommission the plant and that it would have to be kept stable until then. Further, the United States advised Americans to leave an area within 50 miles of the plant, far larger than the 12-mile Japanese evacuation area, because of concerns that the accident was far worse than Japan was reporting.

The Japanese report criticized Prime Minister Naoto Kan for attempting to micromanage its disaster and for not releasing critical information on radiation leaks, thereby creating widespread distrust of authorities among Japanese citizens. The report also concluded that government oversight of nuclear plant safety had been inadequate, ignoring the risk of a tsunami and the need for plant-design renovations, while clinging to a "myth of safety."

Meanwhile, the extraordinary resilience and cohesion of Japanese society helped the nation cope with an unprecedented triple disaster—earthquake, tsunami, and crippled nuclear reactors. Because of these combined events, twenty thousand people died, towns were abandoned, and countless homes and livelihoods were destroyed. And at a baseball stadium in Fukushima, antinuclear protestors gathered to speak out against an energy source that had turned into one of Japan's most divisive and unresolved issues.

By March 2012, only two of Japan's fifty-four nuclear reactors were in operation, a sharp reversal for a country that before 2011 depended on nuclear power for one-third of its energy. This reversal came with a cost because Japanese utility companies were forced to import fossil fuels to maintain a reliable energy supply, leading to higher bills for customers and a lasting trade deficit for the country. Further, more than three hundred thousand people still live as evacuees, either in temporary housing units, in hotels, or in the homes of relatives. A recent *Asahi Shimbun* survey of evacuees found that 40 percent had lost their jobs or other sources of income. Additional surveys show even higher levels of depression and insomnia among Japanese survivors.

Rahna Reiko Rizzuto, author of the memoir *Hiroshima in the Morning*, has discovered three lessons that can be taken from the Fukushima tragedy. First, "government's lie." Signs that the Daiichi reactors had melted down were seen within days, but the Japanese government did not admit it for months. When radiation in food exceeded legal limits and it was pulled off grocery shelves, the Chief Cabinet Secretary said, "Even if people eat these products, there will be no immediate effect."

Rizzuto's second lesson is we are still "gambling" on nuclear power. More than half the world's nuclear energy is produced in Japan, France, and the United States. In the United States, where nuclear plants are between 30 and 40 years old, with aging analog technology, an Associated Press investigation found that three-fourths of these facilities are leaking radioactive tritium. Spent reactor fuel also remains a huge concern. The United States has generated more than 72,000 tons of high-level nuclear waste and has no place to store it. Three-fourths of this waste resides in overcapacity water-cooling pools next to more than one hundred nuclear electric stations in America. Japan is expected to run out of room to store its nuclear waste within 10-20 years.

Ms. Rizzuto further explains that radioactive waste cannot be "neutralized" like other waste products. It is an immediate and deadly threat to human health and has a much longer lifespan than we do (from 500 to 500,000 years). Humanity has never experienced anything that has lasted as long as radioactive poisons will. Rather than focusing our efforts on cleaning up the mess we already have, the United States just approved its first nuclear power plant since the 1970s. The NRC granted its approval over the objection of its own chairperson, Gregory Jaczko, who said that the decision was made "as if Fukushima never happened."

Rizzuto's lesson three is "the ocean cannot wash away our problem." Fukushima has released 169 times the amount of cancer-causing cesium as did the bombing of Hiroshima in 1945. But the ocean is where the true disaster may reside. Water used to cool the Fukushima fuel has been measured at up to 7.5 million times the legal limit for radiation. Further, the Japanese government deliberately dumped 11,500 tons of radioactive water into the ocean during April 2011, calling this act "regrettable and unfortunate." Meanwhile, radiation was discovered in fish and sea water 400 miles away. Thus, Ms. Rizzuto thinks we should abandon nuclear energy entirely. For her and many others, that is the most important lesson of all.

References

Abas, B.
1992 "Justice denied," *Westword*, 7-13 October.
Aleh-zon: An Arizona Journal of Social Ecology.
1991 "Earth first trial," February, 10.
American Sociological Association (ASA).
1993 "Current news." *Environment, Technology and Society* 73: 5.
Arizona Republic
1992 "Pollution raising, health declining, Russians report." 10 October, A7.
Barton, Paul
1994 "Fernald: Study says workers affected," *Cincinnati Enquirer*, 13 April, A1, A5.
Becker, Robert C.
1990 *Cross Currents: The Promise of Electromedicine, The Perils of Electropollution.* Los Angeles: Jeremy P. Tarcher.
Boston Globe
1993 "Radiation testing challenged in 1950," 28 December.
Cable, Sherry, and Michael Benson
1993 "Acting locally: Environmental injustice and the emergence of grass-roots environmental organizations." *Social Problems* 40: 464-477.
CBS News
1991 "Harm's way," *60 Minutes*, 26 May.

Clifford, Mary
1993 "Environmental Systems Company, Inc. In Arizona: Implications for the Social Constructionist Theory and Methodology" (Department of Justice Studies, Arizona State University, Ph.D. dissertation), 6 August.

Cobb, C. E. Jr.
1989 "Living with radiation," *National Geographic*, June, 403-437.

D'Antonio, Michael
1994 "Glow-in-the-dark farmer's tale," *Arizona Republic*, 4 January.

Dricks, Victor
1987 "Chernobyl exposure expected to increase retarded babies 50%," *Phoenix Gazette*, 16 February, A6.

Edelstein, Michael R.
1988 *Contaminated Communities: The Social and Psychological Impacts of Residential Toxic Exposure*. Boulder, CO: Westview.

Feinstein, Mike
1992 *Sixteen Weeks with European Greens: Interviews, Impression, Platforms, and Personalities*. San Pedro, CA: R & E Miles.

Flavin, Christopher
1987 "Reassessing nuclear power." pp. 37-80 in Lester R. Brown et al. (eds.), *State of the World*. New York: Norton.

Foucault, Michel
1977 *Power/Knowledge: Selected Interviews and Other Writings, 1972-1977*. New York: Pantheon.

Freudenburg, William R., and Robert Gramling
1994 "Bureaucratic slippage and failure of agency vigilance: The case of the environmental studies program." *Social Problems* 41: 214-239.

Freudenburg, William R., and Ted I. K. Youn
1993 *Research in Social Problems and Public Policy*. Greenwich, CT: JAI Press.

Gallo, N.
1993 "Nuclear nighmare," *Family Circle*. 2 February, 114-113.

Gould, J. M., and B. A. Goldman
1990 *Deadly Deceit*. New York: Four Walls Eight Windows.

Habermas, Jürgen
1975 *Legitimation Crisis*. Boston: Beacon.

Hardert, Ronald A.
1993 "Public trust and governmental trustworthiness: Nuclear deception at the Fernald, Ohio, weapons plant." *Research in Social Problems and Public Policy* 5: 123-146.

Hardert, Ronald A., Mark Reader, Myron L. Scott, Gerald Moulton, and Alan Goodman.
1989 "A critical theory analysis of nuclear power: The implications of Palo Verde nuclear generating station." *Humanity and Society* 13 (2): 165-186.

Hawkes, Nigel, et al.
1986 *The Worst Accident in the World*. London: William Heinemann and Pan Books.

Herbert, H. Josef
1993 "Atom tests concealed, U.S. admits," *Arizona Republic*, 8 December.

Jones, Ellen and Benjamin L. Woodbury II
1986 "Chernobyl and glasnost." *Problems of Communism*, November-December, 28-30.

Mander, Jerry
1991 *In the Absence of the Sacred*. San Francisco: Sierra Club Books.

Marples, David R.
1988 *The Social Impact of the Chernobyl Disaster*. London: Macmillan.

Massik, Konstantin
1991 "The Chernobyl accident: The heart of the problem." *Impact of Science on Society* 41: 205-210.

Mayo, Anna
1986 "Bitter harvest," New Hampshire [Phoenix, Arizona], 2-8 July, 32 ff. Reprinted from "You wore a tulip," *Village Voice*.

McKinley, Wes and Coran Balkany, Esq.
2004 *The Ambushed Grand Jury*. New York: Apex.

Mishchenko, Yuri and Anatoly Panov
1991 "Chernobyl makes Ukraine want independence," *New York Times*, E16.

Monroe, Kristen R.
1991 "John Donne's people: Explaining differences between rational actors and altruists through cognitive frameworks." *Journal of Politics* 53: 394-433.

Mumford, Lewis
1967 *The Myth of the Machine.* New York: Harcourt, Brace.
New York Times
1990 "A new arena for Soviet nationalism," December.
1991 "Ukrainians ask Gorbachev trial, asserting cover-up at Chernobyl," 12 December, A140.
1993 "U.S. to shine light on dark history of radiation experiments," 18 December.
Oliner, Sam and Pearl Oliner
1988 *The Altruistic Personality.* New York: Free Press.
PBS News
1993 "Secrets of a bomb factory," *Frontline.* One Hour. 26 October.
Perrow, Charles
1984 *Normal Accidents: Living with High Risk Technologies.* New York: Basic Books.
Ra'anan, Uri
1986 "Before and after Chernobyl: Stresses in Soviet leadership." *Orbis* 30: 249-257.
Reader, Frances
1983 "Human Response to Technological Disasters: The Case of Three Mile Island" (Department of Sociology, Arizona State University, unpublished Master's thesis), July.
Reader, Mark, et al
1980 Atom's Eve: Ending the Nuclear Age. New York: McGraw-Hill
Rizzo, Katherine
1993 "U.S. deliberately spread radiation," *Arizona Republic,* 16 December.
Schneider, Keith
1988a "Energy department says it kept secret mishaps at nuclear weapons plant," *New York Times,* 4 October.
1988b "Operators got millions in bonuses despite hazards at atom plants," *New York Times,* 26 October.
Scripps, Howard
1993 "Geographic aspects of the Chernobyl nuclear accident," *Soviet Geography,* September, 504-526.

Sharkansky, Ira
2000 "A state of action may be nasty but is not likely to be a crime." pp. 35-52 in Jeffery Ian Ross (ed.), *Controlling State Crime*. New Brunswick, NJ: Transaction.

Shcherbak, Iurii
1989 *Chernobyl: A Documentary Story*. London: Macmillan.

Shaw, Karen Diane
1992 "Chernobyl and the Crisis of Legitimation in the Former Soviet Union: A Metaphor for the Future? Department of Political Science, Arizona State University (unpublished Master's thesis), December.

Sutherland, Edwin
1983 *White-Collar Crime: The Uncut Version*. New Haven, CT: Yale University Press.

Tsoukalas, Theodore
1994 "Environmental whistleblowers in federal agencies." *Environment, Technology and Society* 75 (Spring): 1-5.

Turco, R. P. et al.
1984 "The climate effects of nuclear war," *Scientific American*, 251 (2). August. U.S. Department of Energy, Environment, Safety and Health
1989 Safety Appraisal of the Program to Control and Monitor Worker Internal Radiation Exposure at the Feed Materials Production Center, Fernald, Ohio, March.

Vognsen, Mary Holasek
1986 Personal Communication.

Voznesenskaya, Julia
1987 *The Star Chernobyl*. London: Quartet Books.

Washington Post
1991 "Chernobyl is all in their heads," National Weekly Edition, 3-9 June, 39.

Welsome, Eileen
1999 *The Plutonium Files*. New York: Delta.

Williams, Frank and Marilyn McShane
1994 *Current Issues in Criminal Justice*. Hamden, CT: Garland.

WISE (World Information Service on Energy News)
1986 "Moscow trust group opposes nuclear power." Communique No. 256, 11 July, 6.

Wolpe, Howard
    1993 The Prosecution of Environmental Crimes at the Department of Energy's Rocky Flats Facility. Subcommittee on Investigations and Oversight, House Committee on Science, Space and Technology, Washington, DC, January 4.

CHAPTER 6

Alternatives to the Nuclear Fuel Cycle

We face a geometric increase in contamination of the environment by nuclear plant emissions. These are radioactive noble gases, radioiodine, tritium, carbon 14, and plutonium and other transuranics. . . . The release of plutonium and other alpha-emitting transuranics will increase by over one hundred times by the year 2020.

—Carl Johnson, MD, Lakewood, Colorado

Introduction

The nuclear fuel cycle has been called a death or cancer machine because throughout the cycle, we are stirring up or manufacturing radioactive elements that are either immediately of potentially damaging to human health in this and future generations. For instance, the radioactive half-life of plutonium-239 is 24,400 years, and there is general consensus that humans will have to isolate this and similar radioactive substances from their lives for as long as is required to safeguard their health and well-being.

Given these characteristics of the fissioned (i.e., "split") atom, people have understandably become skeptical about all "official" claims about its virtues. Thus, this chapter will deal with alternatives to the long-lasting toxicity of the nuclear fuel cycle. Further, the plutonium generated in the fuel cycle is the stuff from which hydrogen bombs are made, and each year every unit of a typical 1,000 megawatt or larger nuclear reactor will produce enough plutonium to make twenty to forty Hiroshima-sized explosives. Since the know-how to make thermonuclear weapons is no longer secret and nuclear fuel cycle components are being sold around the world, it seems only a matter of time before atomic weapons appear in the military arsenals of more nations than presently have them (Snell, 2005: 30-35).

What Can Be Done to Shut Down the Nuclear Fuel Cycle?

As you have learned earlier in this book, the secret of every authoritarian system is secrecy and deception. The key to exercising arbitrary power and total control over a social system is to restrict communication between and among individuals by subdividing information so that only a small portion of the whole truth can be known by any single person. This reductionism is what we have been trying to avoid by focusing our theory and research on the entire nuclear fuel cycle, not just upon Chernobyl, Fernald, and/or Fukushima.

We think that US energy policy should be in accord with the ethic of ecological justice and the guidelines and criteria it suggests. Such policy needs careful development to prevent severe social and economic dislocation. Thus, the authors of this book would support the following:

1. Efforts to conserve energy and to use it more efficiently. Not using energy unnecessarily is the safest and cheapest "energy resource."
2. Publicly funded, energy-conserving projects designed in ways that will provide new skills and jobs for the unemployed and underemployed.
3. Programs to limit fuel consumption which do not rely primarily on raising prices, which places an intolerable burden on the poor, the elderly, and those with fixed incomes.
4. Increased government research and development funding, public and private grants, subsidies, and other incentives to expand the practical application of appropriate energy technologies (based on renewable energy resources), such as solar energy, including wind and water, and geothermal energy.

5. A national energy policy that does not rely on a long-term, large increase in the burning of coal.
6. A national energy policy that will not need to utilize nuclear fission.
7. A continued ban on the commercial processing and use of plutonium as a fuel in the United States and stringent efforts to reach worldwide agreement banning such use of plutonium. Commercial use of plutonium could result in proliferation of nuclear weapons.
8. The rapid development of enforceable regulations to require social and environmental impact statements related to a given technology before it is used and the monitoring and control of its use to prevent social and environmental damage.
9. The US policy that seeks to share appropriate technologies internationally without imposing capital-intensive energy technologies on countries that lack investment capital.
10. Full US cooperation in international efforts to ensure equitable distribution of necessary energy supplies and rapid development and deployment of appropriate technologies based on renewable energy resources, such as solar, wind, geothermal, and moving water.

The governing board of the National Council of Churches of Christ (NCCC) has called upon society to enact energy policy that fosters values of sustainability, fairness, and participation. The institutional church and each of its members, as individuals and as citizens, must challenge traditional modes of energy, thought and behavior. The NCCC governing board urges every Christian, each member communion of the National Council, and the council itself to seek prayerful guidance for a faithful response to the challenge facing all of us globally (Reader, 1980: 246-247).

How to Limit Global Warming Without Turning to Nuclear Power?

First, we must realize that all life on Earth is interconnected (Schumacher, 1973) and that we need a global energy revolution (Dauncey, 2007). Large and small changes will make a difference, even the use of caulking and weather-stripping. Fixing additional leaks and openings with insulation would also help, especially in older homes and businesses. Turning off lights, radios, televisions, and computers when you leave a room will lower your monthly utility bills noticeably. Switching to energy-efficient appliances is another important example of energy conservation, and installing solar panels is a good way to build political will for local energy change (Lovins, 1977).

Second, in the transportation area, we need to drive less and to walk and cycle more. Demanding better mass transit would help, for example, greater use of buses, trains, trams, and carpooling. Not flying unless you have to, and supporting local businesses also reduces global warming. Avoiding drive-through, eating less meat, sharing what you have, and buying less "stuff" would be helpful. Further, we need to invest in quality plant trees, save the rain forests because they produce oxygen, buy eco-certified or recycled timber, eat locally grown organic food, use cloth shopping bags (i.e., refuse plastic), and buy hybrid or plug-in electric vehicles when affordable.

Third, also in the energy conservation area, citizens of the world need to turn up air conditioners, put on sweaters, buy recycled paper, use clotheslines, rake, sweep, shovel, and use self-propelled and solar-electric lawn mowers. Further, fluorescent, coil bulbs last ten times longer than incandescent lamps and use 75 percent less electricity.

Fourth, on a societal and global level, we need to question authority, buy green power produced by solar plants and wind turbines, close down or retrofit coal-burning power plants with "scrubbers" (i.e., CO_2 filters), support climate-friendly politicians, demand stricter emission controls and fuel efficiency on all vehicles, and join the world in supporting the Kyoto Protocol to cut emissions. Finally, all of us need to slow down, think about our environmental futures, find our own voices, and "kiss the carbon years good-bye" (Dauncey, 2007).

On June 7, 2013, Southern California Edison announced it would close its San Onofre nuclear plant between San Diego and Los Angeles rather than fix damaged equipment that critics said could never be safely replaced. The twin reactors were idled in January

2012 when a radiation leak led to the discovery of unusual damage to hundreds of new tubes that carry radioactive water (Blood and Henry, 2013).

The decision to close the San Onofre plant is the latest setback for an industry that seemed poised for growth not long ago. In February 2013, North Carolina-based Duke Energy Corporation decided to close the Crystal River nuclear plant in Florida after workers cracked a concrete containment building during an attempt to upgrade the plant in 2009. The containment building is supposed to prevent the release of gamma radiation, which can penetrate through 10 feet of concrete. An attempt to fix the problem in 2011 resulted in still more cracks (Blood and Henry, 2013). Despite the shutdown, Duke wants its customers to reimburse the company for $1.65 billion in plant investments.

Even working nuclear plants are being scuttled. Dominion Resources, Inc., announced it would close the Kewaunee Power Station in Wisconsin because it could not find a buyer. This decision was said to be based purely on economics as the Great Recession of 2008 trimmed the local demand for electricity. In recent times, only three nuclear construction projects have moved forward, and they are all under financial and political pressure from organizations such as the Affinity Groups listed below.

Affinity Groups Speak to Power

American Civil Liberties Union (ACLU)
    125 Broad Street, 18th floor, New York, NY 10004.
American Friends Service Committee (AFSC)
    1501 Cherry St., Philadelphia, PA 19102.
Beyond Nuclear, www.beyondnuclear.org.
Citizens' Energy Project,
    1413 K St., NW, 8th Floor, Washington, DC 20001.
Clamshell Alliance
    62 Congress St., Portsmouth, NH 03801.
Conservation Foundation
    McDonald Farm, 105404 Knoch Knolls Rd., Naperville, IL 60565.

Federation of American Scientists,
    1725 DeSales St., NW, 9th Floor, Washington, DC 20036.
Fellowship of Reconciliation (FOR),
    Box 271, Nyack, NY 10960.
Friends of the Earth (FOE),
    1100 15th St., NW, 11th Floor, Washington, DC 20005.
Greenpeace, www.greenpeace.org.
Institute of Policy Studies (IPS),
    1112 16th St., NW, Suite 600, Washington, DC 20036.
National Council of Churches (NCCC), Eco-Justice Program Office,
    110 Maryland Ave., NE, Suite 108, Washington, DC 20002.
Natural Resources Defense Council (NRDC),
    40 West 20th St., New York, NY 10011.
Physicians for Social Responsibility,
    1111 14th St., NW, Suite 700, Washington, DC 20005.
Southwest Research and Information Center,
    P.O. Box 4524, Albuquerque, NM 87196.
Syracuse Peace Council,
    2013 Genesee St., 2nd Floor, Syracuse, NY 13210.
Union of Concerned Scientists (UCS),
    Two Battle Square, Cambridge, MA 02138-3780.

References

Blood, Michael R. and Ray Henry. 2013."Sanonofare, Nuclear Plant Closing." *Santa Fe, New Mexican*, June 9.

Dauncey, Guy. 2007. "How to End Global Warming." SCW, Box 6367, Syracuse, NY 13217.

Lovins, Amory B. 1977. *Soft Energy Paths.* Cambridge, MA: Ballinger.

Reader, Mark. 1980. *Atom's Eve: Ending the Nuclear Age.* New York: McGraw-Hill.

Schumacher, E. F. 1973. *Small is Beautiful.* New York: Harper & Row.

Snell, Marilyn Berlin. 2005. "Dangerous Liaisons." *Sierra*, May/June: 30-35.

EPILOGUE

Fernald to Fukushima

Our lives begin to end the day we become silent about things that matter.

—Dr. Martin Luther King Jr.

One hopes that the accident at the Fukushima facility will allow the Japanese to reconnect with the victims of Hiroshima and Nagasaki, to recognize the danger of nuclear power, and to put an end to the illusion of the efficacy of deterrence that is advocated by nuclear powers.

—Kenzaburo Oe

The Fernald saga is the long and detailed story of a rural Ohio farming community that awakened one morning in the fall of 1984 to realize they were living with a nuclear nightmare. It is also the story of a woman who had never spoken out publically, held a press conference, flew on a plane, or organized anything. It took a small group of dedicated women, mostly mothers, to fight for the health and safety of their children and community. These volunteers would bring both the federal government and the DOE to their knees and would help define the real meaning of public involvement. The Fernald Residents found new and unique ways to confront a 40-year-old dirty nuclear production facility (the "Feed Materials Production Center"), shut it down, and literally get it cleaned up, even if it took 23 long years to do so.

Many lessons were learned from how clean is "clean," where the waste should go, drinking water standards, and most of all what the community folks would be willing to endure. It would make Fernald Residents rethink the issue of trucking nuclear and chemical waste across the country, by rail and/or by truck. It would make residents realize and understand the "NIMBY" (not in my backyard) issue and the prospect of storing our nuclear waste on-site, rather than sending it across America.

We learned new terminology in the process of cleaning up Fernald. This included discussion of radiation standards for our air, water, soil, and underground aquifer, as well as state, federal health and safety regulations. It made us realize how important and fragile our children's health and safety were and how better to protect them from environmental threats, both now and in the future.

Numerous journal articles, television news segments, magazines, and newspaper items have been written about Fernald, but precious few books have been published. *Button Up* attempts to correct that omission by discussing Fernald in the context of Chernobyl, TMI, Fukushima, and other accidents, "incidents" and contamination in the global nuclear fuel cycle. This includes social, psychological, environmental, health, and political issues involved in producing both nuclear electric and nuclear weapons.

On a personal note, my own family drank from a uranium-contaminated well and lived directly across the street from the Fernald nightmare. We were right in the middle of this huge controversy. But we learned how important it is to value our community, family, friends, and neighbors. Our activism brought us together in the end.

The greatest lesson learned from Fernald was standing up for what one believes in, fighting for what is right, just keeping one's values, and struggling until the battle is over. When issues touch you personally, it teaches each of us how to take those issues and work with them to make life better for ourselves and others. With each new study, such as this book, more is being taught and learned about Fernald and the nuclear fuel cycle. Fernald has earned its place in nuclear history, mainly because of its local residents, community, and the people whose lives were touched. It was a long, hard-won battle that left many scars, but it created and strengthened numerous friendships, as well.

The nuclear disaster at Fukushima increased the US public concerns about nuclear power and its potential risks. What's emerging in Japan 2 years since the meltdown at Fukushima is a radioactive zone larger than that left by the 1945 atomic bombings at Hiroshima and Nagasaki.

The Union of Concerned Scientists is working to ensure the safety of the US citizens in various ways. They are trying to increase the security of nuclear reactors and of fuel storage sites against terrorist attacks and the theft of nuclear materials from some types of civilian facilities. Citizen knowledge of the dangers of nuclear weapons plants seems to lag behind what the public is coming to know about problems in global nuclear electric. This, too, needs to be rectified.

The 2-year anniversary of the Fukushima tragedy provided an important opportunity to take a hard look at nuclear power and weapons safety in the United States and elsewhere. The UCS report released in 2011, entitled "US Power after Fukushima," provides a list of actions the NRC must take to address serious shortcomings in nuclear plant safety and security that have been evident for years. These recommendations are designed to lessen the chance that a Fukushima-type disaster could happen in the United States.

Dr. Ronald A. Hardert

Included in this list of potential oversight changes is the need to move spent nuclear fuel from on-site cooling pools into dry casks as soon as possible. Finding a permanent and secure location for storing the high-level waste we already have is imperative, as well. Building on these recommendations, UCS continues to educate Congress and the public about improved safety and oversight to prevent another nuclear disaster.

Lisa Crawford, President of Fernald Residents for Environmental
Safety and Health

APPENDIX A

Health Problems Associated with the Nuclear Fuel Cycle—Summary of Relevant Research

Author	Location	Finding
Baron (1984)	14 British nuclear facilities (8 were power plants)	Scattered instances where rates for some types of cancer increased after start-up of a facility.
Black (1984), Craft et al. (1984)	Area near Sellafield (formerly "Windscale," a UK reprocessing plant)	Increased incidence of lymphoid leukemia in children.
Garner et al. (1987)	Town of Seascale near Sellafield	Excess leukemia mortality in children born to mothers who resided in Seascale.
Garner et al. (1987)	Seascale	Excess leukemia mortality in children whose fathers were employed at Sellafield.
Heasman et al. (1986)	Dounreay and Sellafield (North Coast of Scotland)	"Highly significant excess" of leukemia in persons under age 25, 1979-1984.
Darby and Doll (1987)	Dounreay and Sellafield	Childhood leukemia increased in vicinity of both plants.
Roman et al. (1987)	3 nuclear facilities in England (none electric)	Significant increase in leukemia for children under 5 years of age.
Ewings et al. (1989)	Hinkley Point nuclear power station (England)	Increased leukemia and non-Hodgkin's lymphoma among persons under age 25.
Forman et al. (1987)	14 nuclear installations in England and Wales	2 studies found that for those under 25 years, deaths from lymphoid leukemia and brain tumors were more frequent around some of the installations. The effect was stronger for children below 10 years.
Cook-Mozaffari et al. (1989)	Nuclear power stations in England and Wales	Excesses of childhood leukemia and Hodgkin's disease.

Comare Committee (1986, 1988, 1989)	Aldermaston and Burghfield facilities in England and Dounreay in Scotland	Elevated rates of leukemia and some other childhood cancers among children below 10 years in areas near Aldermaston and Burghfield. Incidence of childhood leukemia increased near Dounreay plant.
Stebbins and Voelz (1981)	Los Alamos County, NM	Excess *mortality* from leukemia: *incidence* of leukemia in children not reported.
Crump et al. (1987)	Rocky Flats facility in Colorado	Cancer incidence correlated with proximity to Rocky Flats.
Goldsmith (1989)	Oak Ridge, TN, and Hanford, Washington, weapons plants	Mortality from leukemia among children below age 10 significantly increased near Oak Ridge and Hanford plants during the decade 1950-1959.
Key (1992)	Los Alamos	Thyroid cancer rate from 1980 to 1990 slightly *more* than double the statewide rate for New Mexico. The Los Alamos brain cancer rate was slightly *less* than double the statewide rate.
Wing et al. (1991)	Oak Ridge National Lab	Leukemia mortality elevated in sample of white men hired at Oak Ridge. Between 1943 and 1972, and in workers who had been monitored for internal radioactive contamination.
Sternglass (1981)	Three Mile Island (TMI in PA)	Increased infant mortality and birth defect rates in counties northeast of TMI.
Gould and Goldman (1990)	Chernobyl (1986)	Increased mortality rates in West Germany and as far away as the United States immediately after the Chernobyl disaster.
Gould and Goldman (1990)	Savannah River nuclear weapons facility and TMI	Between 50,000 and 100,000 excess deaths occurred after nuclear releases due to accidents at the Savannah River facility in 1970 and again in TMI in 1979. At both facilities, excess infant deaths from birth defects increased significantly, as did excess death from child cancer and lung cancer.
Wagoner (1980)	Central European uranium mines	1957 epidemic of malignant neoplasms (lung cancer) where 50% of all miners died from radiation.
	All US uranium miners in 1962	Statistically significant excess of cancers among miners in public health reports of 1962.

	All US uranium miners late 1978	3,360 miners studied: 205 died of lung cancer, where only 40 deaths expected.
	Shiprock, NM, hospital	17 lung cancers between 1965 and 1979; 16 were local uranium miners. All were Native Americans and 14 had never smoked.
	Four Corners area (especially NM and Utah)	Altered sex ratio where fewer males were born to miner families. Higher than normal birth defects and infant mortality.
Clapp et al. (1987)	Near Pilgrim power plant	Excess incidence of leukemia in Massachusetts towns near Pilgrim.
Kerber et al. *JAMA*, 270: 17, November 3, 1993	Communities in SW Utah, SE Nevada, and SE Arizona	Excess of thyroid neoplasm (benign and malignant)
Nagtaki et al. *JAMA*, 272: 5, August 3, 1994	Nagasaki, Japan	Significant dose-response relationship observed for solid nodules that include cancer, adenoma, adenomatous goiter, and nodules.
Kuhel and Ward *Lancet*: 346, November 4, 1995	Belarus (Byelorussia)	Childhood thyroid excess after Chernobyl not decreasing. Increase greater among those aged 0-4 and 5-9 at time of accident.
COMMARE Comm.	Sellafield at Columbia, UK	Excess of cancer and leukemia in young people near Sellafield.
Bonn *Lancet*: 347, April 27, 1996	Gomel, near Belarus	Thyroid cancer in children under 14 at more than 100 cases per million per year; normal rate worldwide is 1 child per million.
Nau *Lancet*: 344, August 20, 1994	Ukraine and Byelorussia	Increase in thyroid cases among children almost 400 cases recorded between 1989 and 1993. Short interval between radiation exposure and increased cancer incidence.
Hole *Lancet*: 342, December 11, 1993	Elbmarsh, Germany	5 cases of leukemia in children below 15 years; 1 case of leukemia in patient aged 20, and 1 case of aplastic anemia in a child. Near the largest capacity German boiling water reactor, Krummel
Taylor et al. *Lancet*: 343, 19??	Colorado uranium miners exposed to radon gas	16 lung cancers, 12 of which were squamous cell carcinomas; gross damage to DNA (double-strand breaks)

Stewart report in *Cincinnati Enquirer*, April 13, 1994	Fernald, OH, weapons plant	Significantly elevated lung cancer rates reported in former Fernald nuclear workers.
Johnson (1980)	Rocky Flats (Denver)	Overall cancer rates in men 24% higher than expected; 10% higher than expected for women. 501 excess cases of cancers compared to the unexposed population.
Najarian (1980)	Portsmouth Naval Shipyard (nuclear subs are built, overhauled and fueled)	Workers had nearly twice the expected percentage of cancer deaths and about 5 times the leukemia deaths compared with the general US population of same age at death or with nonnuclear workers at same facility.
Radiation Research (November, 2005)	Ural Mountains of Central Russia	Excess cancers due to chronic exposures to low doses of radiation leaked from a weapons factory 50 years ago.
Science (2005)	Global study of nuclear industry workers	Large-scale study reveals an elevated cancer risk among nuclear workers.
Hardert and Woodward (1998)	Near the Fernald, OH, atomic weapons plant	Ross, Fernald, and Harrison, Ohio, all had elevated crude cancer death rates.
Cincinnati Post (1996)	Fernald weapons plant	Death rate among salaried workers was 161% higher than for the general population.
Pinney, Freyberg, Levine, et al. (2003)	Fernald weapons plant	Prior living within the Fernald exposure domain related to increased urinary system disease. Statistically significant elevation of bladder disease and kidney disease.
Qi (2006)	Fernald nuclear weapons plant	Among the people who drank well water, the nearer they lived to Fernald, the more likely they were to get urinary cancer.
German Register of Child Cancer (August 12, 2007)	Regions near 21 German reactors or former reactors	Children under the age of 5, living near nuclear power stations, contracted leukemia at a rate 60% higher than the national average. Given these findings at every German nuclear power station, a radiation-linked cause is highly likely in every case.

| Yablokov, A., V. Nesterenko, A. Nesterenko in *Chernobyl: Consequences of the Catastrophe for People and the Environment*, New York Academy of Sciences (April 26, 2010) | Northern Hemisphere | Nearly 1 million people around the world died from exposure to radiation released by the 1986 nuclear disaster at Chernobyl reactor. The proportion of children considered healthy born to irradiated parents in Belarus, the Ukraine, and European Russia fell from about 80% healthy to less than 20% since 1986. |

APPENDIX B

Whistle-Blowers, Incidents, Harassment, and Consequences

Whistle-Blowers	Incident	Harassment	Consequence
John Gofman and Arthur Tamplin	Discovered health effects of low-level radiation near nukes	AEC reassigned Tamplin's 12 research assistants, and Gofman lost $250,000 in funding	Gofman radicalized versus AEC
Irwin Bross	Health effects for children of parents exposed to X-rays	NCI grant not renewed; findings not published in government journals	
Thomas Mancuso	Study of radiation health effects	Study terminated by DOE; Mancuso deemed "too old"	Mancuso wanted study to continue
Karl Morgan	Questioned safety of breeder reactors at Nuremburg meetings	Oak Ridge said, "Paper unsuitable for publication"	Morgan became nonnuclear leaving AEC
Sarah Thomas and Linda Mitchell	Questioned safety at Palo Verde nuclear generating station	Thomas given job with higher radiation exposure; Mitchell forced out	Thomas received restitution; Mitchell blackballed from nuclear industry

Gregg Wilkinson	Authored Fed. Study of white-collar crime at Rocky Flats	Pressured by DOE to "suppress or alter his findings"	
Four nuclear workers	Complained about safety and environmental problems	DOE ordered them to see psychiatrists at weapons plant or psychologists	
Casey Ruud and James Simpkin	Exposed safety problems at Hanford	Forced from jobs at Savannah River	
Jackie Brever and Karen Pitts	Told FBI about Rocky Flats problems	Contaminated with radioactive material	Lawsuit filed versus Rockwell International and EG&G, Inc.
Lisa Crawford	Complained to DOE about uranium in her well water near Fernald	Negative reaction from conservatives in Cincinnati	Protects self by leading FRESH group and "being visible"
Rosalie Bertell	Critical of radiation and health problems in nuclear fuel cycle	Windows shot out of her convent in Edmonton, Alberta, Canada	
Political science professor at Arizona State University	Expressed fear of a local nuclear power station	Bulletin board vandalized; classes spied upon	

SUBJECT INDEX

"Accident: A Day's News", 96

Affinity Groups Speak to Power, 152-153

Alternatives to the Nuclear Fuel Cycle, 148-152

Altruists (Oliver and Oliver), 119

American Association for the Advancement of Science (AAAS), 6

Appendix A, Health Problems, 159-163

Appendix B, Whistle—Blowers, 164-165

Arizona Public Service Company, 18

Arizona Republic, 103, 107

Arizona Republic/UPI, 99

Armageddon, 138

Arctic Ocean, 49

Ashai Shimbun Survey, 141

Ashtabula, Ohio Extrusion Plant, 58

Associated Press, 97, 141

Atlantic, 102

Background on Fernald, 37-47

Battelle/Pacific Northwest Laboratories, 67, 121

Belrad Institute in Minsk, 22

Beyond Nuclear, 10

1954 Bikini Atoll Hydrogen Bomb Tests, 106

Biological Effects of Ionizing Radiation (Beir), 32

Bladder cancer, 87

Broomfield Great Western Reservoir and Standley Lake, 45

Cancer, 16,17

Case—study approach, 56

Center for Epigenetics of Common Human Disease, 23

Centers for Disease Control (CDC), 47

Center for Disease Control (CDC), 107

Central Committee of the Soviet Union, 136

Cesium—137, 42

Chelyabinsk Region Children's Hospital, 48

Chernobyl Accident, 100

Chernobylinterinform Information Agency, 21

Chernobyl and Leukemia, 22

Chernobyl (Kiev) Nuclear Electric Station Disaster, x, 3

Christian Science Monitor, 9

Cincinnati Enquirer, 55, 68, 90

Clark County, 46

Clean Water Act, 122

Cleanup Delays at Fernald, 75

Closing the Nuclear Fuel Cycle, 149-150

Columbia Generating Station, 19

Columbia River Contamination, 45

Communist Bloc Countries, 137

Concerned Citizens for Nuclear Safety, 35

27th congress of the Communist Party, 135

Consumer Power, 10

Continuing Health Effects Near Chernobyl, 22-23

Corporate Crime, 123

Crisis of Authority (Habermas), xiii

Crisis of Authority at Fukushima, 140-142

Critical Theory, xii

Crosby Township Senior Center, 25

Crystal River Nuclear Plant, 152

"Deadly Defense", 41

Death in Slow Motion, 105-109

Deception and Secrecy at Fernald, 62-67

Decommissioning Nuclear Facilities, xii

Decommissioning Reactors, 15

Decontamination Projects at Fernald, 25

Delegitimation of Nuclear Regimes, xii

Department of Justice (DOJ), 65

Department of Social Medicine at Birmingham University, UK, 107

Der Spiegel, 108

DOE Weapons complex and Fernald, 57-60

Dominion Resources, Inc., 152

"Downwinders", 69

Duke Energy Corporation, 152

Eastern European Interviews, 132-139

Edgerton, Germestausen & Grier (EG&G), 60

El Independiente (Newspaper), 134

Electric Power Research Institute, 106

Emergence of Grassroots Organizations in the U. S. and Canada, 123-124

Environmental Crimes, 118, 120

Environmental Crime and the US legitimation Crisis, 120-123

Environmental Injustice, 116, 118

1984 Environmental Monitoring Report, 63

EPA Inspector General's Office (IG), 5

EPA's, "Rad Net" monitoring system, 5

"Epigenetics", 23

EPAI Journal, 106.

Exxon Valdez Accident, 96, 122

Faustian Promise, 7

Fernald (OH) Cleanup, 24-25

Fernald Interviews, 85-92

Fernald Residents for Environmental Safety and Health (FRESH), xi, 25

Fernald (OH) Nuclear Weapons Plant, x, 13

Fluor Fernald Corporation, 44

Formal Knowledge, 61

Formation of FRESH (1984), 70

Former Soviet Union, 93, 132

Foucault's Qualitative Methods, 78

Four Corners Area, 69
FRESH, 124
Fukushima Daiichi, 2-4, 140
Fukushima Daini, 2
Fukushima Tragedy, x, 2-6, 140-142
Gaseous Diffusion Plants, 34
German Democratic Republic
(GDR), 101
German Register of Child Cancer, 8
Glasnost Policy, 135
Global Nuclear Fears, 25-27
Global Radiation Fallout, 137
Global Security Newswire, 5
Government Accountability Project,
66
Great Miami River Aquifer, 41
Green World, 139
Hanford Nuclear Plant, 13, 19-20
Health and Global Policy Institute,
6
Hibakusha, 5, 97
Hiroshima and Nagasaki, 14
"Hiroshima in the Morning", 141
Holocaust, 138
Human Genetics Institute of the
Free University of Berlin, 106
IAEA, 109
Idaho National Engineering
Laboratory, 13, 20
"Ideal Speech Community"
(Habermas), xii
Ideological Productions, 61
Inconclusive by Design (Methods),
xii
Independent Investigation
Commission on the
Fukushima Daiichi Nuclear
Accident, 4

Indian Point Nuclear Power Plant,
11
Institutional Crime, 118
International Atomic Energy Agency
(IAEA), 3, 9
International Institute of Concern
for Public Health, 18, 107
International Terrorism, xii
Jefferson County Board of Health,
45
Johns Hopkins Medical School, 23
K-65 Silos at Fernald, 24
Kewaunee Power Station, 152
KGB, 136
Kiev School Children, 130
Kremlin, 135
Kyushu Electric Power, 4
Lake Karachai, 49
Legal Problems at Fernald and
Rocky Flats, 70-73
"Legitimate" Power (i.e., Authority),
60
Legitimation Crisis (Habermas), 76,
123
Legitimation Crisis Theory,
116-118, 123
Lenin's Banner, 95
Lexington Herald-Leader, 11
Lingering Problems with Nuclear
Electric, 18-19
Lisa Crawford and Fernald
Residents (FRESH), 155-158
Logical Fallacy of Reductionism, xii,
26
Long Island Lighting Company, 10
Los Angeles Times, 6
Love Canal, 55
Manhattan Project, 40

Mayak Waste-Tank Explosion, 49
Mechanix Illustrated, 92
Mercury, Nevada, 56
"Methodological Precautions"
    (Foucault), 60
Miami University of Ohio Research,
    66
Misplaced Concreteness, 26
Mkultra and Mkdelta Activity,
    113-115
Mobile, Arizona, 129
Moscow News, 109
Moscow Trust Group, 100, 104,
    134
Mound Nuclear Plant, 86
Mox Nuclear Fuel, 2
National Academy of Sciences, 32
National Atmospheric Deposition
    Samples, 6
National Council of Churches of
    Christ (NCCC), 150
National Energy Policy, 150
National Geographic, 34
National Institute of Occupational
    Health, 17
National Institutes of Health
    (NIH), 23
National Lead of Ohio, 63, 125
Nature, 22
Navaho Nation, 17
NBC Today Show, 97
Nevada Test Site, 14, 69
New Hampshire Electric
    Cooperative, 10
New Pradigm of Appropriate
    Technology, ix
Newsweek, 12

New York Times, 68, 95, 99, 102,
    137
New Yorker, 17
Nimby, 156
NLO (National Lead), 40
Nobel Peace Institute, 94
"Normal" Technological Accidents
    (Perrow), 118
NRC, 141
Nuclear Activism, 124-129
Nuclear Deception on the National
    Level, 67-70
Nuclear Economics, 9-11
Nuclear Fuel Cycle, 8
Nuclear Fuel Cycle Diagram, 1
Nuclear Health Effects, 8-9,
    159-163
Nuclear Interviews , 85-92
Nuclear Nightmares, 92-93
Nuclear Regulatory Commission,
    10, 12, 18
Nuclear Regulatory Failures, xii,
    13-14
Nuclear Secrecy and Deception, xii,
    12-13
Nuclear Skepticism, 103-105
Nuclear Terror, 11-12
Nuclear Theory and Methods,
    60-62
Nuclear Waste Safety Project of
    the Southwest Research and
    Information Center, 13
Nuclear Weapons Issues, 19-22
Nuclear Whistle-Blowers, xiii,
    164-165
Nuke Information Tokyo, 99
Oak Ridge Environmental Peace
    Alliance, 35

Oak Ridge Nuclear Facility, 13, 125
Office of Technology Assessment
    (OTA), 74-75
Ohio Department of Health, 125
Ohio EPA, 125
Ohio Industrial Commission, 63
Ohio Valley Health Problems, 90
Old Paradigm of High Technology,
    ix
Onagawa Nuclear Reactors, 2
Paddy's Run Creek, 41
Paducha (KY) Gaseous Diffusion
    Plant, 21
Palo Verde Nuclear Generating
    Station, 18, 112
Pantex (Texas) Nuclear Plant, 21
PBS News, 121
PCBs (Polychlorinated Biphenyls),
    20
"People", Summer 2009, 37
Perestroika Policies, 108
Personal and Structural
    Contradictions, 129
Phase-ordering Problems, 123, 124
    ff.
Philosophy of Science, xii
Physicians for Social Responsibility,
    7
Portland State University, 107
Portsmouth Uranium Enrichment
    Complex, 86-87
Post-Chernobyl Interviews, 129-130
Plutonium—239, 16, 149
Pravda, 105
Proctor & Gamble, 90
Project Independence, 9-10
Pripyat Region, 94, 130, 132, 136
Profil, 109

Psychosocial Effects of Secrecy, 84
Psychosocial Reactions to the
    Nuclear Age, xii
Public Broadcasting System, 45
Questioning Nuclear Technology,
    6-8
Radiation and Public Health
    Project, 9
Radiation Research, 17
Radioactive Iodine—131 releases,
    68
Radioactive Waste, 14
Radioactive Waste Storage, 16
Radon Gas, 69
Reagan Administration, 138
Rebuild Japan Initiative Foundation,
    140
Regulatory failure, 13-14
Regulatory Failure: Scope and
    Methods, 117-120
Resource Conservation and
    Recovery Act (RCRA), 122
Rockwell International, 59-60, 122
Rocky Flats, 121, 128
Rocky Flats Legal Problems, 72
Rocky Flats Nuclear Plant, 13, 21
Rocky Mountain Peace and Justice
    Center, 36
Safety Practices at Fernald, 62-63
San Onofre Nuclear Plant, 151
Savannah River Nuclear Plant, 13,
    46
Savannah River Reactor Accidents,
    68
2012 Scientific Freedom and
    Responsibility Award, 6
Science Magazine, 17
Seabrook Nuclear Plant, 98

"Seeds of Life" Association, 22

Sierra Magazine, 19

Slowing Global Warming, 150-152

Snake River Palin Aquifer, 20, 46

Southern California Edison, 151

Soviet National Cancer Registry, 22

Soviet Nuclear Waste Legacy, 48-51

Subcommittee on Investigations and Oversights, 121

Subjugated Knowledge, 61-62

Swiss Medical Weekly, 22

Tampere University in Finland, 104

Techa River contamination, 48

Technological Accidents, x

Technological Civilization and the Legitimation Crisis, 113-117

Technological Disaster, 129

Thermonuclear and Biochemical Weapons, 7

Thorium—230, 41

Thorium—230 at Fernald, 64

Time Magazine, 45, 85

Three Mile Island Reactor Accident, 6, 18

"Three Mile Island Revisited", 36

TMI Reactor, 95

Tokyo Electric Power Company (TEPCO), 3, 4, 6

Tom and Yenisey Rivers, 50

Two-headed Calf, 87, 88

Ukraine, Byelorussia, and Moldavia, 134

Ukrainian Parliament, 137

Ukrainian Greens, 134

Union of Concerned Scientists (UCS), 10, 157

U. S. Department of Agriculture, 66

U. S. Department of Energy, x, 21, 125-127

U.S. Department of Energy, Office of Legacy Management, 155

U.S. Department of Labor, 18

U.S. Environmental Protection Agency (USEPA), 5

U.S. Geological Survey, 43

U.S. Nuclear Weapons Complex, 14, 33-37

U.S. Nuclear Weapons Complex, xi

U.S. Materials Production Plants, 34

U.S. Nuclear Research Laboratories, 34

"U.S. Power After Fukushima" (Report), 157

University of Waterloo, 39

Vermont Law School's Institute for Energy And Environment, 10

Village Voice, 95

Vitrification, 24

Voices from Chernobyl, 93-103

Voices from Fernald, 84-85

Washington Post, 137

Washington Public Power System, 10

Waste Central Specialists, 24

Waste Isolation Pilot Project (WIPP), 20

Western European Interviews, 130-132

Westinghouse Nuclear Reactors, 26

Westinghouse Materials Company of Ohio, 39

What Happens if We Continue to Go Nuclear, 74

WIPP Project, 126
World Health Organization
    (WHO), 9
World Information Service on
    Energy (WISE), 94
World Trade Center, 11
Wormwood, 138-139
Yucca Mountain, 13-14, 20

NAME INDEX

Ahmed, Salahuddin, 99
Alexievich, Svetlana, 111
Alven, Hannes, 26
Amano, Yukiya, 3
Archer, Victor E., 69
Arthur, Daniel J., 62
Bailie, Tom, 68, 120
Baker, Debbie, 37
Benson, Michael, 115, 116, 117, 118, 120, 122, 123, 124, 125, 126, 127, 128
Bernal, V., 31
Bertell, Rosalie, 18, 31, 107
Blain, Michael, 46
Bohr, Niels, 57
Bradford, Peter, 10
Bradley, General Omar N., ix
Bush, George W., 17, 44
Cable, Sherry, 115, 116, 117, 118, 120, 122, 123, 124, 125, 126, 127,128
Caldicott, Helen, 15, 16, 27, 31, 59
Carpenter, Tom, 66, 67
Carter, Jimmy, 18
Celebrezze, Anthony J. Jr., 72
Chambliss, William, 56
Chesley, Stanley, 71, 72
Chun, Rene, 11,12
Clarke, Lee, 56
Clayton, Mark, 9, 10

Cook, Renae, 67
Cooper, Mark, 10
Commoner, Barry, 27
Crawford, Ken, 70, 76
Crawford, Lisa, xi, 25, 44, 64, 70, 76, 78, 85,124, 125, 126, 158
Doj, Pal, 99
Douglas, Mary, 56
Duffy, Leo, 77
Edelstein, Michael, 76
Einstein, Albert, 8, 55
Etzkowitz, Henry, 56
Finesilver, Sherman, 73, 121
Finsterbusch, Kurt, 76, 77
Foucault, Michel, xi, 60, 61, 62, 66, 78, 112
Fradkin, P. L., 31
Frazier, Timothy A., 17
Funabashi, Yokhi, 4
Gale, Robert, 107
Gibbs, Lois, 78
Glenn, John, 75
Goffman, Erving, 62
Gofman, John, 31, 106
Gorbachev, Mikhail, 108, 134, 135, 136, 137, 138, 139
Habermas, Jürgen. xi, xiii, 112, 116, 117, 123
Hamilton, Thomas, 106

Hancock, Don, 13, 14, 78, 126, 127
Henderson, Hazel, 27
Hirsh, Daniel, 5
Hoffman, Eva, 96
Honicker, Clifford, 70
Hueper, William C., 69
Iwanow, Woloymjir, 134
Jaczko, Gregory, 141
Johannson, Olaf, 95
Johnson, Carl, 45, 49, 104,148
Kan, Naoto, 140
Kaplan, Abraham, xii
Kelly, Herbert, 63
Kennedy Jr., Robert F., 84
King Jr., Martin Luther, 155
Kline, Allan, 70
Kovalevska, Liubora Oleksandrivna, 132
Kurokawa, Kiyoshi, 6
LaDuke, Winona, 31
Legason, Valery, 108, 109
Levine, Adeline Gordon, 55
Lifton, Robert Jay, 96, 97
Lipsky, Jon, 36
Liukkonen, Marjo, 104
Lovins, Amory, 27
Lovins, Hunter, 27
Luken, Thomas A., 65
Magnuson, E., 68
Makhijani, Arjun, 31, 65, 75
Malloy, Brian, 94
Manning, Peter, 56
Matsumura, Naoto, 4, 5
Mayo, Anna, 95
Meyer, Kathy, 70
Mills, C. Wright, xi
Montanari, Fred W., 64

Moore, LeRoy, 36
Mumford, Lewis, 27
Munson, Linda, 67
Mushkatel, Alvin, 75, 76
Newman, Penny, 78
Nixon, Richard, 9
Norton, Michael, 72, 73, 121
Obama, Barack, 10, 14, 17
Oe, Kenzaburo, 155
Perrow, Charles, 56
Pijawka, David, 75, 76
Reader, Mark, xi, xv, 6, 7, 93, 118
Reid, William K., 35
Renshaw, Scott, 62
Resnikoff, Marvin, 43
Rhodes, Richard, 31
Rizzuto, Rahna Reiko, 141, 142
Roselle, Louise, 63, 64
Ross, Jeffery, 56
Russell, Dick, 58
Ruttenber, Jim, 107
Ryzhkov, Yevgeny, 49
Scarce, Rik, 114
Schell, Jonathon, 98
Schroeder, Pat, 73
Schumacher, E. F., 27, 68
Shcherbak, Iurii, 138
Simon, Paul, 70
Slater, Mary Jo, 102
Slotkin, Louis, 70
Smale, Alison, 97
Sorokin, Pitirim, xiii
Sperling, Karl, 106
Spiegel, S. Arthur, 71, 72
Steinem, Gloria, 97
Stewart, Alice 43, 44, 107
Stockton, Pete, 12
Striesand, Barbara, 97

Tschernosenko, Vladimir, 109
Udall, Stewart, 31
Virilio, Paul, 1
Vogel,Richard, 106
Voznesenskaya, Julia, 136, 138
Waldthaler, Kirsten, 93
Watkins, James, 72
Weart, Spencer R., 92, 93
Weidner, Robert B., 67
Whitehead, Alford North, xii
Wildovsky, Aaron, 56
Wilkinson, G. S., 59
Wolf, Christa, 96
Wolpe, Howard, 121, 122, 123
Yablokov, Alexey, 8, 9
Yelstin, Boris, 131
Zeh, Foster, 11, 12
Zhukovskaya, Elena, 48
Zinser, Charles, 38, 39
Zinser, Louis, 39